GOLF'S
BOOK OF
FIRSTS

GOLF'S
BOOK OF
FIRSTS

ADAM SHERMAN

READON
PUBLICATIONS
INCORPORATED

8241 KEELE STREET, UNITS 9-10
CONCORD, ONTARIO L4K 1Z5

Published by World Publications Group, Inc.
455 Somerset Avenue
North Dighton, MA 02764
www.wrldpub.com

ISBN 1-57215-396-2

Interior book design by Beth A. Crowell
Cover design by Jack Tom
Edited by Sharyn Rosart and Emily Zelner
A special thanks to Joel Carino for his contributions to this book.

Printed and bound in China by SNP Leefung Printers Limited.

1 2 3 4 5   06 05 03 02

PAGE 2: Golfer Bobby Jones follows his shot,
September 14, 1926.

THIS PAGE: Babe Zaharias driving on the course
at the Los Angeles Golf Tournament in 1938.

CONTENTS

CHAPTER 1

The Game

ave you ever played a round of golf with someone whose swing evoked images of a caveman slugging a club against a stone? While there aren't any cave drawings that show our prehistoric ancestors swinging golf clubs, surely there was an early human who discovered that a stick or branch could be used as an extension of the arm.

Perhaps he also realized that he could take out his frustrations and amuse himself at once by whacking a stone with his instrument. And then what if he added a contraption to the end of the stick and created a pushing mechanism for encouraging the rock to end up at a designated spot? Sounds like prehistoric golf.

There have been so many club-and-ball or stick-and-ball games described throughout history that speculation as to when golf originated has virtually no bounds. Some historians have traced the roots of golf to ancient Rome, where *panganica*, a game that employed a bent stick and a ball made from leather filled with feathers (see "The First Golf Balls," page 12) apparently was popular with the country folk in the early days of the Roman Empire.

The next incarnation of golf showed up in England while Edward III was in power. In *cambuca* or *cambuta*, a curved stick, similar to the one use in *paganica*, was used along with a ball made of feathers. The ball, researchers believe, was thrown toward a set spot on the ground. In 1363, the game, along with cockfighting and football, was banned on all holidays (there was a penalty of imprisonment if one didn't comply) so that all able-bodied men could sharpen their training shooting the bow and arrow. Less than a century later, a Scottish Act of Parliament applied a ban on the sport for the same reasons.

It is probably *cambuca* that is illustrated in a stained-glass window on the eastern façade of the Cathedral of Gloucester, which dates from the mid-fourteenth century. The representation shows a headless figure holding a curved stick as if he were swinging a curved club. The figure is fixed on a yellow ball, which is against a green background. The image bears a striking resemblance to what we know as golf, but it is more likely a depiction of *cambuca* which was played in England at the time.

By the late Middle Ages, a game called *jeu de mail* or *paille maille* had become popular in France. It was played with balls and mallets along a course roughly a half-mile long; the winner of the game was the player who required the least number of strokes to reach the chosen mark. Belgians enjoyed a similar sport known as *chole*. Although any of these sports may have influenced our game, the likeliest possible forerunner of golf came from Holland, where the Dutch played a stick-and-ball game called *kolven* — and by the 1300s, trade between the Scots and the Dutch was brisk.

LEFT: For all intents and purposes, this is where golf first took shape: The Swilken Bridge crosses over to the 18th hole on the Old Golf Course at St. Andrews.

What is indisputable is that it was in Scotland that the various influences came together and developed into the game we know today as golf. Scottish fishermen may have brought the game's forerunners to their homeland. To cure their boredom and buoy their spirits as they returned from sea across the links (the sandy areas between sea and village), the fishermen were known to swat pebbles or stones with pieces of driftwood. No doubt the rocks occasionally fell into the plentiful rabbit holes, bringing the essential element of modern golf into play — the hole.

The coastline of Scotland — with its plentiful sand dunes, shrubbery and other vegetation that anchored the windswept land, and scrubby grass fit only for sheep and rabbits — supplied the Scots with on-the-spot golf courses.

Those unsuspecting sheep may have played a role — albeit a passive one — in the emergence of golf. Their sheep required little supervision, so the shepherds often left the main responsibilities for their flocks to their dogs, allowing the shepherds time to work on their game.

By the 1400s, golf was widely played in Scotland. In 1457, it was banned as being against the national interest. King James II felt that the nation's defense was being compromised because golf was preferred to archery training, the latter being crucial for defense against the English.

The ban was reconfirmed in 1470 and again in 1491. Finally, in 1502, with the signing of the Treaty of Glasgow between England and Scotland, the ban was lifted. Also in 1502, James IV made the first recorded purchase of golf equipment (see "The First Golf Clubs," page 10). James is known to have played a match against the Earl of Bothwell in 1503. He was the first of many royal golfers, and evidently encouraged his subjects to play.

Catherine of Aragon, the first wife of Henry VIII (and luckier than most, because she escaped the block) wrote to Cardinal Wolsey that "all his [the king's] subjects are very glad, Master Almoner, I thank God, to be busy with golf, for they take it for pastime."

Today it has become a pastime beloved by players the world over. How did the equipment and rules we play by develop? Read on to find out.

The First Set of Golf Clubs
Perth, Scotland

1502

BELOW: Jamie Anderson of Forgan's Golf Shop at St. Andrews checking over a set of clubs in 1938, some of them almost 100 years old.

OPPOSITE: The original championship clubs of clubmaker and golf professional Old Tom Morris, along with some of his tools for shaping the clubs and stuffing "featheries."

Although there must be a history of early golfers carving clubs from tree branches or hiring woodworkers to create them, the earliest written mention of a set of clubs is a commission from King James IV of Scotland to a bow-maker in Perth in 1502 for a set of clubs. His great grandson, James I of England, was sufficiently enthusiastic about the game to appoint a royal clubmaker in 1603, a bowyer named William Mayne.

A set of clubs during that period was made up of "long-noses" used for driving, "grassed drivers" for mid-range shots, "spoons" for short-range shots, "niblicks" (similar to today's wedges), and a putting "cleek." The poem "The Goff," written by Thomas Matheson in 1743, describes one set:

Of finest ash, Castalio's shaft was made:
Pondrous with lead and fenced with horn the head.
The work of Dickson who in Letha dwells
And in the art of making clubs excels.

In this era, the clubs were made of two pieces. The heads were made from tough woods such as beech, holly, or blackthorn. Shafts were typically made from ash or hazel. Leather straps bound the two pieces together, or they were glued and dipped in pitch to strengthen the join.

Making golf clubs was laborious, and the clubs often broke. In the mid-1800s, clubmakers found that imported hickory from the New World was a better material in terms both of strength and straightness of grain. Hickory shafts wrapped with leather grips became popular around the same time as the guttie ball. In the days of the featherie, the club could damage the ball; once the guttie was introduced, the opposite was true, and clubs changed accordingly.

As early as 1750, some clubmakers had used metal to construct clubfaces. These clubs were considered to be the first irons. Forged by ironsmiths, also known as cleekmakers, the early irons were heavy and unwieldy. "Cleek marks," imprinted by the makers, can be seen on antique clubs. Through the 1800s, clubmakers continued to experiment with metals, eventually working with aluminum and steel.

Steel shafts, along with persimmon club heads, became popular in the early days of the twentieth century, just as golf began to surge in popularity. Innovations abounded, including the center-shafted club (1892), F. W. Brewster's "Simplex" torpedo club (1897), and Arthur F. Knight's controversial Schenectady putter (1903). Mass-produced clubs and balls made the game accessible to far greater numbers. In 1895 William Mills produced a set of aluminum "woods." Five years

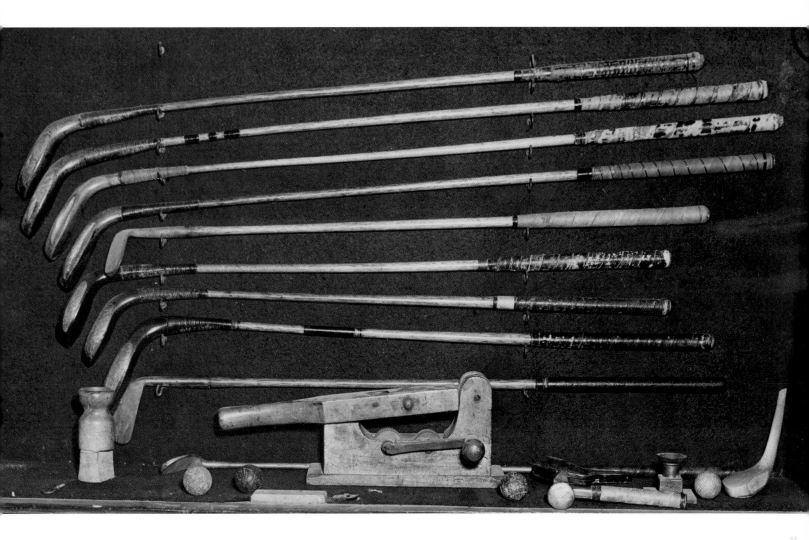

later, Spalding & Bros. used drop forging to mass-produce metal club heads. In the early 1900s, designers realized that a grooved-face club put more backspin on the ball, giving it more distance. It was around this time that the modern golf ball displaced the solid guttie.

In 1939, there were so many choices that the R&A felt it necessary to introduce the "fourteen-club rule," to prevent golfers from using an inordinate number of clubs. At this time, the use of such names as cleek, mid-iron, brassie, and jigger, had given way to the modern numbering system — with the exception of the driver. The lofts of the clubs and their shaft lengths also became standardized with the number system.

The technological innovations of World War II affected golf club development as synthetic and composite materials became available. In the late 1950s, Karsten Solheim developed the "Ping" putter, using heel- and toe-weighting in order to increase the sweet spot. The casting method of manufacturing club heads was introduced in 1963. The Shakespeare Sporting Goods Company developed the first graphite shaft, developed in 1969. Considerably stronger, but also about thirty percent lighter than steel, the graphite shaft gave the golfer more clubhead speed with less effort.

Taylor-Made was the first company to manufacture metal woods. Only recently have they become more popular than persimmon woods. One of the most successful clubs in history is Callaway's oversized wood, the "Big Bertha," which was introduced in 1991. Woods with titanium heads and graphite shafts are among the newest trends, as clubs continue to evolve.

Club Monikers
Then and Now

Modern	Old
1 wood	Driver
2	Brassie
3	Spoon
4	Cleek
1 iron	Driving Iron
2	Mid Iron
3	Mid Mashie
4	Mashie Iron
5	Mashie
6	Spade Mashie
7	Mashie Niblick
8	Lofting Iron
9	Niblick
Putter	Putter

The First Golf Balls Not Made of Wood

Scotland

1618

Golf as we know it today was first played with a leather-covered ball stuffed with goose or chicken feathers. Although one documented reference tells of a man named John Daly playing with a wooden ball (possibly beechwood) in 1550, and leather-covered balls packed with wool may also have been in use, the origins of today's ball lie in the "featherie." This feather-stuffed ball debuted in 1618, along with the probable origins of the term, "knocking the stuffing out of the ball."

To make this handcrafted ball, several pieces of sturdy leather — usually taken from the hide of a horse or bull — were tightly sewed together, leaving a small opening for inserting the filling. The casing was then inverted to allow the stuffing to be placed inside. The stuffing, which had had been boiled and softened, was laboriously packed into the casing before the final stitches were made.

Once packed and sewn, the leather shrank and the feathers expanded to create a hardened ball. The solid form, in a shape that resembled a cube, was then hammered into roundness and coated with paint. The finished ball was then stamped with the ballmaker's mark.

The featherie's quality varied according to the skill of the craftsman. Unfortunately, the time-consuming manner of construction meant that ballmakers could produce an average of only four balls a day, which in turn meant that a ball was quite expensive. Indeed, a single ball could cost more than a club did.

The featherie wasn't a distance ball, usually falling shy of 200 yards (180m). And because of its unforgiving constitution, the feathery often damaged the wooden clubs of the time. Still, for all its detriments and shortcomings, the featherie lasted well over two hundred years, until the new technologies of the nineteenth century made the impractical ball obsolete.

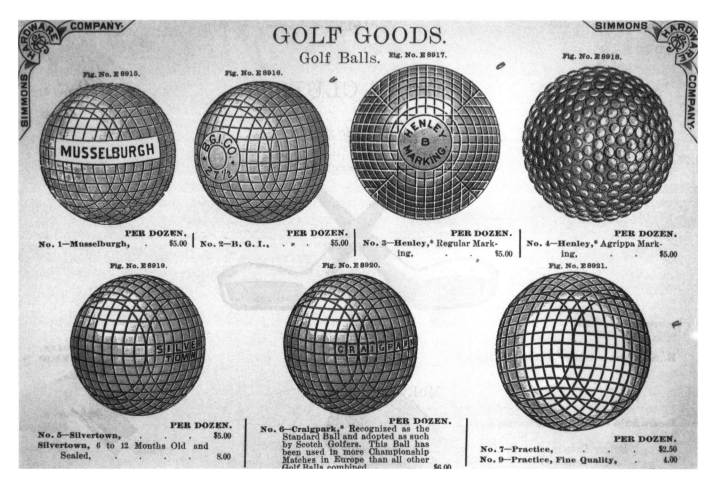

The adoption of the gutta-percha ball, or "Guttie," in 1848 not only put an end to the featherie's reign but actually affected the way the game was played. The first guttie is believed to have been made by Reverend Dr. Robert Adams Paterson of St. Andrews, Scotland, who assembled the ball from gutta-percha packing material that had been used to pad a statue shipped to him from Singapore. Gutta-percha is the evaporated milky juice extracted from one of several trees found in Malaysia. When extracted from the tree, and boiled in water, gutta-percha became soft and malleable. Gutties were handmade by rolling the softened, hot stuff between two flat boards to form a ball, which dried hard. The sturdiness of the guttie and its resistance to water, not to mention its lower cost than the featherie, led to a surge in golf's popularity as more people could afford to play the game.

Though some traditionalists resisted using the new ball (Allan Roberston, a brilliant golfer and a member of a featherie-making family was one well-known foe), ultimately progress could not be stopped — and then came the Hammer Head Percha.

As often as necessity leads to invention, so does chance. The gutta-percha ball, though hard, was subject to denting, and most golfers would smooth out their dinged balls after a game by boiling them, then rolling the hot balls on a smoothing board. It was not long before some keen-eyed golfers noticed that their nicked or indented balls flew more truly than the smooth gutta. Some of them experimented with deliberately whacking the softened ball all over with a sharp-edged hammer. The result was the hand-hammered gutta. The dents created tiny air pockets and decreased wind resistance, which allowed the ball to travel a greater distance. Later, pushing the technological envelope further, balls were made in iron molds or ball presses that created built-in patterns or markings. These balls rewarded their inventors by tending to go even farther.

The First Rules of Golf
The Gentlemen of Leith

1744

OPPOSITE: This is a copy of golf's original rules, which provided guidance and uniformity to a game that was beginning to develop.

A group of golfers from the Scottish burgh of Leith (near Edinburgh) persuaded the city fathers of Edinburgh to donate a silver trophy to be awarded to the winner of the Royal and Ancient Championship. Several clubs participated in the championship, with the new clubs looking to the Gentlemen of Leith for guidance in developing a uniform set of rules. This prompted members from Leith to pen the first written rules of golf (facsimile opposite), which numbered thirteen:

- *You must Tee your Ball within a Club's length of the Hole.*
- *Your Tee must be upon the Ground.*
- *You are not to change the Ball which you Strike off the Tee.*
- *You are not to remove Stones, Bones or any Break Club for the sake of playing your Ball, Except upon the fair Green & that only within a Club's length of your Ball.*
- *If your Ball comes upon watter, or any Wattery Filth, you are at liberty to take out your Ball & bring it behind the hazard and Tee it, you may play it with any Club and allow your Adversary a Stroke for so getting out your Ball.*
- *If your Balls be found anywhere touching one another, You are to lift the first Ball, till you play the last.*
- *At Holling, you are to play your Ball honestly for the Hole, and, not to play upon your Adversary's ball, not lying in your way to the Hole.*
- *If you shou'd lose your Ball, by its being taken up, or any other way, you are to go back to the Spot where you struck last & drop another Ball, And allow your Adversary a Stroke for the misfortune.*
- *No man at Holling his Ball, is to be allowed to mark his way to the Hole with his Club, or with anything else.*
- *If a Ball be stopp'd by any person, Horse, Dog, or any thing else, The Ball so stopp'd must be play'd where it lyes.*
- *If you draw your Club, in order to Strike and proceed so far in the Stroke, as to be bringing down your Club; if then, your Club shall break, in, any way, it is to be Accounted a Stroke.*
- *He, whose Ball lyes farthest from the Hole, is obliged to play first.*
- *Neither Trench, Ditch, or Dyke, made for the preservation of the Links, nor the Scholar's Holes or the Soldier's Lines, Shall be accounted a Hazard; But the Ball is to be taken out / Teed / and play'd with any Iron Club.*

These first rules set no standard number of holes; indeed, the first tournament had but five — long — holes. The rules, including number of holes, that came to be considered standard were ultimately to be set down by the Royal and Ancient Golf Club of St. Andrews.

By the early part of the twentieth century, the Royal and Ancient and the USGA, the governing body of golf in the United States, both applied the same basic rules; however, they made separate interpretations of decisions.

These differences were more or less resolved at a special conference in 1951, which was also attended by representatives from Canada and Australia. Moreover, both bodies agreed they would meet every four years to review the rules, and they set up a Joint Decisions Committee to establish uniformity whenever possible. A book of Decisions on the Rules, which first appeared in 1984, is jointly published by the two organizations and revised annually.

Articles & Laws in Playing the Golf

1. You must Tee your Ball within a Club length of the Hole

2. Your Tee must be upon the Ground

3. You are not to change the Ball which you Stroke off the Tee

4. You are not to remove Stones, Bones or any Break Club for the Sake of playing your Ball, Except upon the fair Green and that only within a Club length of your Ball.

5. If your Ball comes among Water, or any Watery filth, You are at Liberty to take out Your Ball, and bringing it behind the Hazard and Teeing it, You may play it with any Club, and allow Your Adversary a Stroke, for so getting out Your Ball.

6. If Your Balls be found any where touching one another, You are to lift the first Ball, till you play the last.

7. At Holeing, you are to play Your Ball honestly for the Hole, and not to play upon Your Adversary's Ball, not lying in your way to the Hole.

8. If you should lose Your Ball, by its being taken Up, or any other way, You are to go back to the Spot, where you Struck last, and drop another Ball, and Allow Your Adversary a Stroke for the Misfortune.

9. No Man at Holeing his Ball, is to be Allowed to mark his way to the Hole with his Club or any thing else.

10. If a Ball be Stop'd by any person, Horse, Dog, or any thing else, the Ball so Stop'd must be played where it lyes.

11. If you draw Your Club in Order to Strike, and proceed so far in the Stroke as to be bringing down Your Club; if then Your Club shall break, in any way, it is to be Accounted a Stroke.

12. He, whose Ball lyes furthest from the Hole is Obliged to play first.

13. Neither Trench, Ditch, or Dyke made for the preservation of

The First Official Golf Club
The Royal and Ancient Golf Club of St. Andrews

ST. ANDREWS, SCOTLAND

1871

BELOW: America's Tiger Woods tees off toward The Royal and Ancient Golf Club during the first round of the British Open Championships at the Old Course in St. Andrews, Scotland.

OPPOSITE: Golfers play through a hole in front of The Royal and Ancient Golf Club of St. Andrews in 1905.

The founding of the Royal and Ancient in 1754 marked golf's official introduction into the world of organized sport, when a group of enthusiasts banded together to form the Society of St. Andrews Golfers. In 1834, the society was granted the title Royal and Ancient by King William IV.

Although golf had been popular in Scotland at least since the 1400s, it was not until these twenty-two "Noblemen and Gentlemen of the Kingdom of Fife" came together that an official club was formed, and a set of rules written.

The founding document of the club features a list of the founders, and the following account of the society's goals:

The Noblemen and Gentlemen above named being admired of the ancient and healthful exercise of the Golf, and at the same time having the interest and prosperity of the ancient city of St. Andrews at heart, being the Alma Mater of the Golf, did in the year of our Lord 1754 contribute for a Silver club having a St. Andrew engraved on the head thereof to be played for on the Links of St. Andrews upon the fourteenth day of May said year, and yearly in time coming subject to the conditions and regulations following.

The Royal and Ancient Golf Club of St. Andrews has been held in the highest regard around the world ever since its inception. The basic rules it set for the game came to be accepted and adopted throughout the entire world as golf gained widespread popularity.

The minutes from some of the first meetings held at R&A, as well as other Scottish golf clubs during that period, showed that the members played hard, drank hard, and, most important-ly, enjoyed the time spent taking part in a game that was not altogether clearly defined.

Members paid off their golf bets and club penalties in wine, usually "claret," or Bordeaux, and the prize for the British Open became known as the "Claret Jug."

The R&A remains a private golf club for the elite of the golfing world, and also serves as the governing body of golf throughout the world outside the United States and Mexico. It runs major championships, including the British Open, and reviews the rules of golf.

The R&A does not own the Old Course, as the links at St. Andrews are known — the land is public and owned by the people of the town of St. Andrews. However, the R&A has maintained a long and close connection with those responsible for the links. For many years, this was the Town Council. Then in 1974, with the abolition of the St. Andrews Town Council, a new Act of Parliament created the St. Andrews Links Trust, an independent and charitable body charged with the operation and protection of the courses.

The relationship remains close today, as three R&A members are appointed members on the Board of the Trustees and the Links Management Committee of St. Andrews Links Trust.

The First Golf Course
The Old Course at St. Andrews

ST. ANDREWS, SCOTLAND

1764

BELOW: A golfer at the Old Course at St. Andrews in 1865 readies himself for a shot as onlookers study his approach.

OPPOSITE: A portrait depicts golf being played along the water at St. Andrews in 1860.

This is where it all began: golf has been played at the Old Course for more than four hundred years. And while over those years there have been a few manmade enhancements to the course, its spectacular natural beauty remains unchanged.

The links were an area of sandy, scrubby land that linked the farms to the sea; inappropriate for agriculture, they proved perfect for golf. The Old Course represents the classic seaside links, although the sea is seldom seen, save at the first and last holes, where the vista of St. Andrews Bay elicits gasps.

Although "The Links" form Scotland's oldest and most venerable golf course, St. Andrews' history also includes a brief period as a rabbit farm — starting in 1797, when the bankrupt town of St. Andrews sold the land to local merchants. It was not until 1821 that a local landowner and keen golfer named James Cheape bought the land and restored it to golf. In 1854, the R&A clubhouse was erected. In 1894, the St. Andrews town council reacquired the links from the Cheape family. The New Course was built in 1895, followed by the Jubilee Course in 1897, and the Eden Course in 1914.

The Old Course originally consisted of twenty-two holes, eleven front and eleven back. Upon completing a hole, a player teed up his ball within two club lengths of the previous hole, using a handful of sand scooped out from the hole to form a tee. In 1764, the Society of St. Andrews Golfers, which later became the Royal and Ancient Golf Club, decided that some holes were too short and so they combined them. This reduced the course to eighteen holes in total, and created what became the standard round of golf throughout the world.

When "Old Tom" Morris, the first professional greenkeeper, created a separate green for the first hole, it became possible to play the course in an anti-clockwise direction, rather than clockwise, as had previously been the norm. For many years, the course was played clockwise and anti-clockwise on alternate weeks, but now the anti-clockwise, or right-hand, circuit has

become the accepted direction. Many of the course's more than one hundred bunkers, however, are clearly designed to catch the wayward shots of golfers playing the course on the left-hand circuit.

By the mid-nineteenth century, overcrowding meant that golfers in different matches would find themselves playing to the same hole, but from opposite directions. To relieve the congestion, two holes were cut on each green, and those for the first nine were equipped with a white flag while those for the second nine were marked by a red flag — the origin of the famous double greens.

The course is recognized for its imposing physical attributes, including 112 bunkers, some of which are particularly notable, for example, "Strath" on the short 11th, "Hell" on the short 11th, and the "Road Bunker" on the 17th, also known as the "Road Hole" because a road, which is in play runs hard against the back edge of the green.

Numerous major championships take place regularly on the Links. The most important is the British Open, which was first held on the Old Course in 1873, and was played there for the twenty-sixth time in 2000.

For the 2000 Open, the yardage of five Championship holes was increased by a total of just over 180 yards (162m) to bring the course length to 7,115 yards (6,402.5m). New tees were put in but otherwise the course was essentially the same for 2000 winner Tiger Woods as it was for Tom Kidd when he won the first Open over the Old Course in 1873.

The First Golf Club in North America
The Royal Montreal Golf Club

MONTREAL, QUEBEC

1873

BELOW: Original Royal Montreal charter members gather for a meeting in 1873.

OPPOSITE: North America's first golf clubhouse provides a friendly companion to its 18th hole.

The nineteenth century brought a wave of Scottish immigrants to the United States and Canada; along with their hopes and dreams, many of them brought a passion for golf.

The first golf club in North America was established in Montreal, Quebec, in 1873. Alexander Dennistoun, a Scot who had originally settled in Peterborough, Ontario, gathered seven of his fellow expatriates and local Montreal businessmen together to found what was first known as the Montreal Club, shortly thereafter renamed the Royal Montreal. It was the first course anywhere to obtain approval from Queen Victoria to use the "Royal" prefix.

Establishment of the Royal Montreal Golf Club was quickly followed by the creation of a club in Quebec City, now known as The Royal Quebec Club, in 1875. These two clubs played the first interclub match in Canada, at Cove Fields in 1876. The Toronto Golf Club came into being in 1881; the Victoria Golf Club was formed in British Columbia in 1893. By 1895, ten clubs had become the founding members of the Royal Canadian Golf Association. In 1898, the RCGA and the USGA arranged the first international matches between Canada and the United States.

It was not just the wave of Scottish immigrants that made Canada especially ripe to be the home of the first golf club in North America. Just before the turn of the 19th century, there was a tremendous boom of the game of golf in Canada. There were several contributing factors. The change from a rural society to urban centers began to take hold, and urban living improved the chances for outdoor activities. Easier and enhanced modes of transportation also had an impact on the increased popularity of golf. The completion of the Canadian National Railways and urban trains and trolleys gave people a convenient and accessible means to get where they wanted to

NOTMAN & SON.

go. Oddly enough, however, it may have been the invention of the bicycle that played the largest role in establishing golf. It was during this decade that the restrictions of the Victorian era woman began to fall away. The bicycle provided middle-class women with an easy form of unaccompanied transport, and as a result, directly or indirectly, influenced the introduction of women into the sport in the 1890s.

The first women's clubs — three of them — were all established in 1891, in Montreal, Quebec, and Toronto. The Royal Montreal hosted the first Canadian Amateur Ladies' Championship that year. It was the first club in North America to permit women to become members. Golf was increasingly popular among women, and membership grew rapidly, later helping to sustain the clubs through the years of World War I when male membership decreased dramatically.

In 1904 the Royal Montreal hosted the first-ever Canadian Open, and J.H. Oke won the inaugural event, which had a purse of $60. Since then the club has hosted eight more championships: 1908 (Albert Murray); 1913 (Albert Murray); 1926 (Macdonald Smith); 1950 (Jim Ferrier); 1975 (Tom Weiskopf); 1980 (Bob Gilder); and 1997 (Steve Jones), when Jones edged out Greg Norman on the Club's Blue Course. The Open Championship returned to Royal Montreal in 2001, marking the ninth time it has been held at the esteemed club; Scott Verplank was the winner.

The Royal Montreal comprises the Blue, Red, and Black (Dixie) Courses, with the Black being a 9-holer for juniors and beginners. The Blue Course hosts the Bell Canadian Open, and has water on six of the last nine holes.

The First Recorded Game Played on City-Owned Land Under Local Government Authority

The William J. Devine Golf Course at Franklin Park

1890

BELOW: The William J. Devine Golf Course at Franklin Park, shown here in its infancy, is America's second oldest golf course.

OPPOSITE: Hall of Fame baseball player George Wright, shown here in a plaque commemorating him during his years with the Cincinnati Red Stockings, was one of the driving forces behind the birth of public golf in the United States.

George Wright, whose first game was baseball — he was a Hall-of-Famer — was the catalyst for the birth of public golf. Wright, who was also a partner in a Boston sporting goods store, believed that anyone with an interest in the game of golf should be able to participate. Until his efforts made it possible, however, golf was reserved for private institutions only.

On a bone-numbingly cold day in December 1890, Wright and a few of his friends played the first public golf game on the Franklin Park grounds. The ground had frozen so solidly that they had to use a pickax to dig holes for the game.

Although it is the second oldest public course in the United States — the Bronx's Van Cortlandt Park is the oldest — Franklin Park was the first place where folks who didn't have a private golf club membership could get a game.

It was Wright, and later Willie Campbell, a transplanted Scottish golfer who was influential in shaping the course, who enabled the masses to participate in a sport that was beginning to flourish all over North America.

Wright was introduced to golf through friends with whom he played cricket; when he noticed golf equipment in an English sporting goods catalog, Wright ordered a dozen clubs and balls for his store. To his dismay, the goods didn't come with any instructions for playing the game.

It wasn't until he displayed the clubs in the window of his store that the former baseball star would receive the necessary tutelage in the game that was beginning to pique his interest. A

Scottsman who noticed the clubs in the window, stopped by the store to inquire where the nearest golf course would be. Wright, who now had the equipment to play but scant knowledge of the sport, asked the man to explain the game in more detail to him. The man obliged enthusiastically, giving Wright a thorough golf lesson — from its principles to the order of play. He also sketched Wright a layout of a typical golf course, and, after returning to Scotland, sent him a rulebook and a set of clubs.

Now thoroughly engaged and eager to play, Wright began scouting potential sites in Franklin Park. Upon asking a park policeman about using the grounds for golf, he was told he'd have to apply for a permit from the city. Wright then arranged a meeting with Fredrick Law Olmsted, the park's chief architect, to discuss playing golf on the park's grounds. Olmsted wasn't thrilled at the prospect of having golf matches intrude on his pristine parkland, perhaps to damage his carefully laid out landscaping and shrubbery. Despite Olmsted's disapproval, however, Wright was given a permit for an "experimental" round of golf.

On December 10, Wright and his buddies set out on what was to be the first attempt to play golf on public property. They arranged nine holes and played them twice. They marked the course, which was removed at the day's end, with 3-foot (1m) high flying scraps of red flannel, which served as flagsticks.

Six years passed between Wright's first Franklin Park foray and the establishment by the city of a permanent golf ground, but Wright's efforts on behalf of public golf were the crucial first steps in making the game accessible to all.

GEORGE WRIGHT
STAR OF BASEBALL'S FIRST
PROFESSIONAL TEAM, THE
CINCINNATI RED STOCKINGS OF 1869.
GREAT SHORTSTOP AND CAPTAIN OF
CHAMPION BOSTONS IN NATIONAL
LEAGUE'S PIONEER YEARS.

The First Permanent Course Laid Out on City Parkland
Van Cortlandt Park

BRONX, NEW YORK

1895

ABOVE: Golfers await their turn at the first tee in 1915 at Van Cortlandt Park.

OPPOSITE: The interior of Van Cortlandt Park's Golf Club in 1906.

The New York City Parks Department considered it an experiment. Would a city-owned golf course prove successful, and perhaps offer a blueprint for other cities that suffered from the lack of a decent public course for urbanites? A nineteenth-century businessman named Gustav H. Schwab, who resided in what is now known as University Heights, had put forth the original proposal for a course in the Bronx. Mr. Schwab — and a number of his golf-playing friends — were equally anxious to begin the experiment.

Though Schwab et al had originally hoped for a private club, when the petition to the New York City Park Commissioners was accepted, it was for a public course. In the summer of 1895, a nine-hole course on 55 acres (22ha) of the park opened.

The course proved such a draw that one year later, in 1900, it had to be remodeled to eliminate congestion and prevent accidents. There was one golf clubhouse to service the needs of the players, and it had to be expanded several times to accommodate more golfers.

The ninth hole — at 580 yards (522m) long — was a conversation piece. The tradition of extreme length has endured at Van Cortlandt in the years since. The present course includes two 600-yard (540m) par fives, one on the second hole, which is 625 yards (562.5m), and the other, on the twelfth, at 605 yards (544.5m). They are situated side by side, with the twelfth hole re-creating the original ninth.

In 1899, Scottish course architect Tom Bendelow expanded the course to eighteen holes on 120 acres (40ha). In 1904, 184 lockers were added to the building, and, in 1907, another 96. The number of permits to use the links rose from 1,892 for the entire year in 1899 to an average of 5,000 a week in 1920. Van Cortlandt rapidly became a favorite of celebrities, too. Baseball players Babe Ruth and Christy Mathewson relaxed there, along with numerous politicians and civic leaders of the day.

In the 1930s, players arrived by railroad, using the old Putnam line — or by subway, exiting the station within one block of the first tee. A season's pass cost $10 and a weekend round took six hours — typically, after a five-hour wait.

During the same period, the construction of the Henry Hudson Parkway and its junction with the extension of Mosholu Parkway inside Van Cortlandt Park wiped out six holes of the Van Cortlandt Course. Other holes were eliminated with the construction of the Major Deegan Expressway through the park in the mid-1950s. The lost holes were rebuilt, though some were in a marsh. The tenth hole in particular, which was located

between the marshland and the railroad tracks, was often muddy. Still, a decade later in the1960s, the course remained so feverishly popular that it stayed open throughout the winter. Not only did other cities follow the lead of New York, but also within the Bronx itself, other courses sprang up. As early as 1914, the Mosholu Golf Course opened in the southeast section of Van Cortlandt Park. Later, the Pelham and Split Rock courses were made available in Pelham Bay Park. More recently, Jack Nicklaus' company has designed a new Ferry Point Park course, just south of the Whitestone Bridge.

During the tenure of Mayor Rudy Giuliani, Van Cortlandt completed a major renovation. The nearly $4 million dollars' worth improvements in Van Cortlandt Park included the rebuilding of twenty new tee boxes, thirteen new bunkers, two lakes, and significant redesign of the fairways and rough. At the same time, the pro shop was renovated and updated.

The First Golf Club in Australia
Royal Melbourne Golf Club

MELBOURNE, AUSTRALIA

1891

BELOW: Royal Melbourne Golf Club's original members huddled outside their newly formed club in 1891.

OPPOSITE: Two white benches, which sit in the rough along the fairway of the 8th hole at Australia's first golf club, provide both a resting place and a possible hindrance for golfers.

The nineteenth century saw golf become popular around the world; Australia, with so many settlers of Scottish origin, was no exception. Records describe games in Tasmania in the 1820s, and later in Melbourne (1847), Adelaide (1870), and Sydney (1882).

Clubs were formed but not until the establishment of the Melbourne Golf Club, which has existed continuously from 1891, did they show much staying power. Melbourne is regarded as the first golf club in Australia. Queen Victoria accorded the club the privilege of the prefix "Royal" in 1895.

Not surprisingly, it was a group of Scottish immigrants who had the idea for the club in the first place. What initially attracted John Bruce, Tom Finlay, and Hugh Playfair, from St. Andrews, as well as William Knox and Tom Brentnall, who had played golf at Musselburgh, to Melbourne? It was the same quality that made the Royal and Ancient Club of St. Andrews so spectacular: a gorgeous site blessed by unsurpassed natural beauty.

After numerous discussions, a formal meeting was held at Scott's Hotel in Melbourne on May 22, 1891, to establish the Melbourne Golf Club. Seventy-three founding members chose Sir James McBain as president, and John Bruce as captain.

By the end of June they had chosen a plot of land suitable for an 18-hole course that Finlay laid out near the Caulfield Railway Station. On July 4, 1891, six weeks after the club's founding, the Caulfield course opened. John Bruce drove the first ball and won the first match — against Hugh Playfair.

The course at Caufield lasted until 1901. By that time, the city's growing population meant that houses were encroaching on the clubhouse; the Royal Melbourne Council decided it

would be best to move the course. It would move one more time, for the same reason (to Sandringham) before its final move to the place where it currently resides, in Black Rock.

After selling the land at Sandringham in 1926, the Club Council decided to ask for expert advice on the design of the new course. They tapped the expertise of one of the world's pre-eminent golf architects, Dr. Alistair McKenzie, designer of Augusta National in Georgia, the site of the Masters Tournament.

McKenzie was called in to create the championship course at Royal Melbourne during his visit there in 1926. Alex Russell, the 1924 Australian Open Champion, laid out the East Course, while McKenzie laid out the West.

In 1931 the Club moved to Black Rock and the West Course was opened for play. With Alex Russell as architect and Mick Morcom in charge of construction, the East Course was laid out during 1930-31 and was ready for play late in 1932.

The Composite Course came into being in 1959 when Royal Melbourne was asked to hold the Canada Cup (now the World Cup). It was decided to use twelve holes from the West Course and six holes from the East Course to keep the new Composite Course within the confines of the home paddock. Since then, the Composite Course has been the site for many international tournaments and is regularly rated in the world's top ten courses.

The First Wooden Golf Tee
Golf-Playing Dentist-Inventors

BOSTON, MASSACHUSETTS

1899

BELOW: While golfer Harry Lauder is clearly being outrageous as he tees off on top of a pile of dirt, in his time tees weren't made yet, so, one would have to form a small mound of dirt or sand, on which to tee up.

OPPOSITE: Australian Joe Kirkwood was an excellent golfer who won many professional tournaments in Australia, Europe, and America. However, he was best known for his trick shots, like hitting a ball teed up in his caddy's mouth.

Before there were golf tees, golfers had to invent a way to steady their balls for tee-off. One early solution was to dig out sand from near the green to create a mound with it. Then they would position the ball at the top of the mound, making sure it was secure enough to be hit.

To assist golfers in creating the right effect before teeing off, it became customary to place an iron sandbox, which contained dense sand, nearby. This enabled caddies or players to form a cone of sand for the ball to rest on without having to dig up the grounds. The box also served to mark the driving area.

At the turn of the nineteenth century, an African-American dentist and avid golfer named George F. Grant invented the golf tee. (Dr. Grant was not only one of the first African-American golfers in post-Civil War America, but also was one of the first to practice dentistry. The son of slaves, he graduated from Harvard Dental School with honors.)

Dr. Grant was not the most skillful golfer; still, he enjoyed the recreational aspects of the game. His motivation in creating the tee came not only from a desire to improve his drive, but also from a professional desire to keep things sanitary. In short, Dr. Grant disliked getting dirt on his hands at the tee; he also found the method of pinching damp sand into a launching pad for teeing up a ball to be inconsistent, tedious, and messy.

Thus inspired, Dr. Grant used his professional know-how to improve the game, developing the first wooden tee. In 1899, the U.S. Patent Office granted patent 638,920 to George F. Grant of Boston. But Dr. Grant was more innovator than businessman, and never marketed his invention. He gave some of the tees to friends and playing partners, but the majority of them were squirreled away at his residence. When he died in 1910, his invention apparently died with him. His concept, although revolutionary for its time, was not widely accepted.

It was not until 1922 that another golf-playing dentist, Dr. William Lowell of Maplewood, New Jersey, re-invented the wooden tee. Lowell had originally used gutta percha, but the tee proved too easily broken. The wooden tee, made from white birch, was much sturdier. Lowell's invention, patented in 1924, was called the "Reddy Tee," so named for its color (he painted them red) and convenience. The Reddy Tees received invaluable promotion when Walter Hagen and Joe Kirkwood used them during their world exhibition tour, tucking fresh ones behind their ears to keep them handy.

Within a few years of the Reddy Tee's invention, numerous competing brands were available — although Lowell's patent application had not been specific enough to ensure him exclusivity, it is his Reddy Tee that we recognize today as the model for the modern golf tee.

The First Sand Wedge
Gene Sarazen

February 27, 1902 – May 13, 1999

1902

CAREER HIGHLIGHTS
U.S. Open: 1922, 1932;
USPGA: 1922, 1923, 1933;
British Open: 1932; U.S.
Masters: 1935; USPGA
Seniors: 1954, 1958.

Winner of 38 U.S. Tour
Events, 1922-24,

Ryder Cup Team: 1927-37

USPGA Hall of Fame
1974, Old Tom Morris
Award 1988, Ben Hogan
Award 1992.

RIGHT: Gene Sarazen (left),
creator of the sand wedge,
poses with motion picture
producer Howard Hughes
(who was the inspiration for
the club) as Sarazen boards
a train in Los Angeles in
1933.

OPPOSITE: Sarazen
working out of a sand trap
during the 1974 Masters
Tournament.

t was a flight in billionaire Howard Hughes' private jet that
inspired Gene Sarazen's brilliant idea. It was a simple cause-
and-effect moment: when a plane takes off, its tail goes down.
Sarazen figured the same principle could apply in golf.
"I was trying to make myself a club that would drive the ball
up as I drove the club head down," Sarazen said. "When a pilot
wants to take off, he doesn't raise the tail of his plane, he lowers
it. Accordingly, I was lowering the tail or sole of my niblick to
produce a club whose face would come up from the sand as
the sole made contact with the sand."

He built the prototype in a small machine shop in New
Port Richey, Florida, in 1931. He started carrying it in his golf
bag in 1932. Before the creation of the club, many golfers had
a difficult time pulling out from the bunker.

Striving for the complete game, Sarazen modified his 9-iron
with a heavy-soled flange that permitted him to strike down
on the ball and give it some loft. With his sand wedge, which
became a standard club for all players, he was soon an excellent
trap player.

Gene's foray into golf began at age eight, when he became a golf caddy at the Larchmont Country Club near his home in Harrison, New York. It didn't take long before he had an opportunity to play. At the same time, he helped his father, Federico Saracini, who was a carpenter, build barracks for the war effort as the United States entered World War I. It was there at Fort Slocum that Sarazen did all the nail hammering that strengthened his wrists, and in turn, his golf game.

After the completion of the project, his father moved the family to Bridgeport, Connecticut. Gene, continuing to hone his golf skills, started to practice and play at Beardsley Park, the local public course.

One day, Sarazen and a local professional each holed their tee shots on the same par-three hole. Gene was pleased to read about what he had done in the town's newspaper but wasn't too thrilled at how his name looked in print. Saracini, he thought, was too long for a golfer, and Eugene seemed like a good name for a violinist. He wanted a crisp-sounding name that rolled off the tongue — like Jim Barnes or Chick Evans — two luminaries of contemporary golf, and so he shortened his name to Gene Sarazen.

Though not very tall, Sarazen was built like a fireplug and swung a mighty stick — his drives would consistently carry 240 to 250 yards (225m) when he was on. And he most certainly was, especially in the early years of his career. By the time he reached his twenty-second birthday, he already had three major titles to his credit, with the U.S. Open and USPGA in 1922 and the USPGA in 1923. However, Sarazen hit a dry spell after that; almost nine years passed before he landed another major title. The emergence of the legendary Bobby Jones didn't help Sarazen's cause.

In addition to creating the sand wedge, Sarazen managed several other notable "firsts." He became the first player to win two majors in the same year (the U.S. Open and the USPGA Championship in 1922); upon winning the 1935 U.S. Masters, he became the first golfer to collect all four professional titles; and in 1935, he played what is possibly the single most famous golf stroke of all time. At that year's Masters, trailing Craig Wood by three strokes after 72 holes, Sarazen holed out at the par-5 fifteenth hole with a 4-wood over the water for an albatross-2 (also known as a double eagle). The next day he won the tournament.

The First Golf Clubhouse in the United States

YONKERS, NEW YORK

1888

BELOW: Golfers Harry Holbrook, A. Kinnan, John B. Upham, and John Reid survey the land at the St. Andrew's Golf Club in Yonkers founded by Reid in 1888. A couple of very junior caddies assist them.

At the beginning of 1887, few Americans had ever even heard of the game of golf.

That was soon to change, as the passion New Yorker Robert Lockhart had for golf soon infected his friends, and later his countrymen as well. Lockhart had played the links at Musselburgh, Scotland, before immigrating to the United States. The transplanted linen merchant returned to his native country frequently on business, but always found time for sport.

After one trip to his homeland, Lockhart had returned to New York with tennis balls and racquets, but the new game met with resistance from his friends. Not to be discouraged, however, during the pivotal visit in summer of 1887, Lockhart visited the St. Andrews' shop of Old Tom Morris, the resident clubmaker, where he ordered six clubs and two dozen gutta-percha balls, all to be shipped to his home in New York City.

When the clubs and balls arrived in the fall, Lockhart and his sons carried the equipment over to a meadow on the west side of the city, where they tried it out. Their interest in the sport soon waned, however, and Lockhart passed on the equipment to his friend John Reid. A few months later, Reid and five friends (excluding Lockhart) tried out the new game in a pas-

ture near Reid's home in Yonkers, New York. There weren't enough clubs to go around, and the men got in only one round on the small three-hole course they created on the pasture. Still, all six were hooked, and soon became obsessed with the game.

Unfortunately, their infatuation for golf would be put temporarily on hold when a blizzard in the beginning of 1888 blanketed the pasture with three feet (1m) of snow. Patiently, they waited until the weather warmed and the snow melted, then returned to the pasture. It became obvious very soon, however, that the baby course was not only unsuitable for so many players, but also no longer adequate for the long-term pursuit of competence in playing golf.

The next move was to a 30-acre (12ha) meadow owned by a German butcher named John C. Shotts, where Reid and friends set up a new six-hole course. On November 14, 1888, five of the six original players held a meeting at Reid's home, and decided to form a "golf club."

The club would solidify the bond they had as friends and as golfers, and it would also be a way to acquire funds for course maintenance. Each of the original six players became an officer of the club, with Reid elected president.

They didn't forget Lockhart, either, electing him the club's first member. Theirs was the first golf club in the United States; they chose to name it after the famous original links course on the east coast of Scotland. The club distinguished itself from its namesake by using an apostrophe (St. Andrew's, not St. Andrews).

In 1892, a road expansion forced the St. Andrew's Golf Club to move to a new location. The site they chose was a nearby 34-acre (13.6ha) apple orchard. Set high on a hill, the property offered scenic views of the Hudson River and neighboring New Jersey.

The new six-hole, 1,500-yard (1,350m) golf course, which snaked its way through the orchard, took a whole day to design. Perhaps its most distinctive feature was a large apple tree that stood between the first tee and the last green. Whenever the members of the club went out to play, the tree was where they hung their coats, placed their lunch boxes, and had their spirits. And it was for that reason that John Reid, John Upham, Henry Tallmadge, Harry Holbrook, King Putman, and Alexander Kinnan will always be known as the "Apple Tree Gang."

By 1900, there were nearly 2,000 golf clubs in the United States — just twelve years after Lockhart's imported equipment inspired John Reid and his five friends to form St. Andrew's.

The First Dimpled Golf Ball

William Taylor

LEICESTER, ENGLAND

1905

Golf's popularity increased dramatically as the twentieth century dawned, and technological advances were rapid. One revolutionary change in equipment took the game to new heights — literally.

It began with a casual player named Coburn Haskell, who was inspired by a balled-up clump of rubber bands. With a friend who was an employee of the Ohio-based Goodrich Tire and Rubber Company, he created the "Haskell," a one-piece rubber-cored ball. The new ball resembled the guttie, but it gave the average golfer an extra twenty yards (18m) from the tee. Sandy Herd was the only man in the field to play with a Haskell at the 1902 British Open at Royal Liverpool. He beat the great Harry Vardon and James Braid by a single shot to capture the tournament, and showed people how much distance a ball of this caliber could travel. The ball proved so effective that just a year later it was in wide use.

The Haskell balls were constructed from a solid rubber core wrapped in rubber thread and encased in a gutta-percha sphere. Soon after their introduction, the invention of a thread-winding machine allowed the Haskell balls to be mass-produced, which made them widely affordable.

Another marked change in the way the ball looked and traveled occurred in 1905, when English engineer William Taylor invented the first dimpled golf ball. Taylor, who had built a successful business in lensmaking, turned his attention toward golf after his doctor suggested that he needed to find a relaxing hobby.

Professionals in the sport had already realized that scuffed or nicked balls would travel farther than new ones, which were smooth. When a smooth ball sails through the air, it leaves a big pocket of low-pressure air in its wake. That creates drag, which slows it down.

Dimples, conversely, reduce drag by creating turbulence in the air around the ball. The air follows the curve of the ball around the back of it. The result is a smaller wake and less drag. It soon became a standard to produce balls with various types of patterns and irregularities on them as a way of increasing a ball's flight.

Taylor, taking a scientific tack, built a glass chamber in which smoke was blown over alternatively patterned ball surfaces. He then carefully studied the eddies and vortices of the ball surfaces which resulted.

He concluded that existing patterns were not ideal and developed a pattern consisting of regularly spaced indentations over the entire surface of the ball — the resulting ball soon became famous as the "dimple ball."

Taylor didn't stop there. He went on to invent a special engraving machine for making the molds for these revolutionary golf balls.

In 1906, Goodrich tried to compete with the Haskell by introducing a "pneumatic" ball with compressed air at its core, but its unfortunate tendency to explode caused the company to recall it shortly afterward.

Not until 1972, when Spalding introduced the first two-piece ball, were there any further significant innovations in ball technology.

The First Mention of Birdie
Abe Smith

ATLANTIC CITY, NEW JERSEY

1903

BELOW: Jack Nicklaus rejoices after holing a birdie on the 17th to carry him to victory at the 1986 U.S. Masters at Augusta.

OPPOSITE: Mark O'Meara celebrates after sinking a birdie putt on the 18th to win the 1998 U.S. Masters with a score of 279 at the Augusta National, Georgia.

Every time Judy Rankin let fly for the flagstick and had a chance for a short approach with the hopes of beating par, the former LGPA professional would look for a "birdie" in the sky.

Though one would assume the term birdie originated via the resemblance of a soaring ball to a bird's flight, it actually hails from elsewhere. In nineteenth-century American slang, the term "bird" was applied to anyone or anything considered superior or wonderful.

Casual golfer Abe Smith was the first to apply the phrase to golf while playing a foursome at the Atlantic City Country Club in New Jersey. He hit an excellent shot that left him inches away from the hole. As told in H.B. Martin's book *Fifty Years of American Golf,* Smith related: "My ball…came to rest within six inches of the cup. I said, 'that was a bird of a shot… I suggest that when one of us plays a hole in one under par he receive double compensation.' The other two agreed and we began right away, just as soon as the next one came, to call it a 'birdie.'"

One of the most spectacular birdie flurries in golf history came from 1959 Masters champion Art Wall, who birdied five of the last six holes to come from behind and win by one stroke.

He holed from 15 feet (4.5m) at the thirteenth, from 20 feet (6m) at fourteen, two-putted for a birdie at fifteen, sank another 15-footer on the seventeenth, and rolled one in from 12 feet (3.6m) at the last. Starting the day six shots behind the leader, Wall's incredible rally led him to shoot a final round of 66 to win the match.

Winning birdies were also featured at the amazing finale of the 1961 USPGA Championship at Olympia Fields. On the last three greens of regulation play, Jerry Barber nailed putts of 20 feet (6m) for birdie, 40 feet (12m) for par, and 60 feet (18m) for birdie to tie Don January, who had held a four-stroke lead over Barber with just three strokes to play. Barber had nine single-putt greens in his final round of 70. He then won the following day's playoff 67-68.

The First Book on the
Mental Side of the Game
The Mystery of Golf

1908

OPPOSITE: Tiger Woods of the U.S. lines up a putt on the 11th green during the first round at the 130th British Open Championship at Royal Lytham and St. Annes Golf Club, Lancashire, England.

ABOVE: Phil Mickelson contemplates his double bogey at the 16th hole during the first round of the U.S. Open at The Shinnecock Hills Golf Club in Southampton, New York. The errant shot cost Mickelson the early lead – and his concentration.

"Golf is like faith: it is the substance of things hoped for, the evidence of things not seen."

Arnold Haultain's description of golf was written in the early half of the twentieth century, but it unquestionably nails the mystery golfers have wrestled with since the game was invented. How do you explain a game that at the end of the day leaves you with something that isn't necessarily tangible, but is nevertheless real?

That telling line from Haultain crystallizes the essence of his book, *The Mystery of Golf*. Originally published in 1908, it was the first publication to ruminate on the troubled and often perplexing region known as the golfer's mind, and to grapple with the constant and fanatical hold the game has over it. Frequently philosophical in his approach, Haultain suggested there were only three great puzzles to have truly obsessed the minds of men: metaphysics, golf, and the female heart.

Haultain, a Canadian belles-lettrest, fancied himself an expert golfer. His classic tome explores the incurable romance of golf. *The Mystery of Golf* examines the confounding sport from all angles, detouring from the technical, in which the author considers the elements of the perfect swing, to the abstract, in which he attempts to explain the psychology of a sport in which the true opponent is not another player, but oneself.

In 1996, novelist John Updike, no stranger to the curious allure of golf, wrote of Haultain's work, "The book's core is pure gold… Haultain goes to the heart of golf's peculiar lovability and enduring fascination."

Though much has changed in the game since Haultain wrote his book, it endures because it captures the essence of the sport's hold on its enthusiasts. Proof? *The Mystery of Golf* remains in print today, almost a century after it was first published.

The First Professional Greenkeeper

"Old Tom" Morris

1865

magine the wonderment Old Tom Morris might feel
upon being introduced to the latest advances in greenkeep-
ing. During his heyday in the 1800s, there were no precision
mowers, high-tech irrigation systems, or specially bred
disease-resistant strains of turf grass.

Old Tom's main tools were a bit more low-tech —
sheep, which shaped the greens and fairways by chewing on
the grass — and scythes, which were swung by the greenkeeper
himself. Before there were sprinklers or hoses of any kind, Old
Tom used to irrigate the greens and fairways by digging deep
into the ground next to each green until he hit water. Then he
would lower a bucket into the well and pull up the water —
this is how he irrigated the entire course.

Before Morris was made official greenkeeper at St. Andrews
in 1865, the only mention of such comes from the minutes of
The Royal Burgess Golfing Society, which note in 1774 that a boy
had been engaged as "our cady" and "greenskeeper," for which he
was paid six shillings per quarter year and a suit of clothes.

However, by the mid-1800s, a council comprising two
members from each of five area clubs was appointed to take
responsibility for the course and find someone "to make holes,
look after the flags, and mend the turf." A professional golfer
was to be employed as a servant of the club and the entire
charge of the course was to be entrusted to him.

Already a well-known golfer when he took the job at
St. Andrews, Morris had apprenticed with ballmaker Allan
Robertson (with whom he often played at St. Andrews), and
had been groundskeeper at Prestwick. He had been involved
in organizing the first British Open (in which he finished second
to Willie Park) and competed in every Open until 1896, taking
the championship in 1861, 1862, 1864, and 1867. His 1862
win was by a margin of thirteen strokes, a record that stood
until Tiger Woods broke it with fifteen in 2000.

As greenkeeper, Morris' responsibilities included sustaining
the putting greens, repairing them when necessary, and making
new holes. A part-time assistant was expected to help out two
days a week. The newly appointed chief of the links was paid a
salary of seventy pounds a year. It must have been a satisfactory
arrangement, because Morris
would continue in the job until
1903, when he retired after
forty years as greenkeeper.

Despite the passage of
time, some of the maintenance
practices that Old Tom devised
are still in use today. Among
his innovations are metal cups
for firming up the holes and
"top-dressing" bare spots with
sand to encourage the growth
of grass. Morris is also famous
for laying out courses all over
Britain, including Muirfield, Royal
Dornoch, Lahinch, and Royal
County Down. He died in 1908,
at the advanced age of eighty-
seven.

The First Mention of Bogey
Major Charles Wellman

GREAT YARMOUTH CLUB, ENGLAND

1890

BELOW: Payne Stewart recoils as his putt rims out on the eighth hole for a bogey during the second round of the U.S. Open at Oakland Hills Country Club in Bloomfield Hills, Michigan, in 1996.

OPPOSITE: Vijay Singh blows an insect away from his ball before finishing his hole with a bogey on the 17th during the 3rd round of the 1995 NEC World Series of Golf in Akron, Ohio.

The term bogey comes from a song popular in the United Kingdom in the early 1890s, called "The Bogey Man" (later known as "The Colonel Bogey March"). The subject of the song was an elusive figure who hid in the shadows, hence the lyric: "I'm the Bogey Man, catch me if you can." (*Bogle or bogie* is an old Scottish word for ghost.)

It is believed that a Major Charles Wellman, while playing against par, described his failure to get to that mark as "getting caught by the bogey man." The members of the club soon began referring to an imaginary new member, Colonel Bogey, who would always shoot even par.

As the game spread to North America, the definition of "bogey" changed to mean a score of one over par on a hole. It also came to be used to describe stroke-play tournaments — as a result, in the early rulebooks there is often a section called "Bogey Competitions."

The record for the most bogies, as well as that for the highest score ever recorded at a single hole, goes to Ray Ainsely. It was the 1938 U.S. Open at Cherry Hills in Denver, Colorado. Ainsely was 15 over par when he reached the sixteenth hole, where he drove his ball into a rapidly moving creek altogether too close to the green.

Following it into the water, Ainsely made numerous valiant attempts to get the sunken ball back onto dry land, but the water kept pushing his ball downstream and farther away from the hole. He eventually managed to loft it out of the creek, and from there, Ainsley knocked it onto the fairway, played it onto the green, and, on his nineteenth stroke, single-putted. When asked afterwards why he hadn't taken a drop under penalty, Ainsley said that he thought he had to play the ball as it lay.

He missed the cut by 17 shots with rounds of 76 and 96.

More bogey-mania came at the 1969 Masters, when Charles Coody, with the tournament seemingly in hand, blew it by bogeying the final three holes to finish two strokes behind winner George Archer. A decade later at Augusta, Ed Sneed suffered a similar fate after he closed with three successive bogies before losing a playoff to Fuzzy Zoeller.

The First Golf Book to Use High-Speed Sequence Photography

Picture Analysis of Golf Strokes

1919

Jim Barnes was a man of many firsts. Known as "Long Jim" because of his height, reed-thin frame, and long shots, Barnes won four major championships in an era best known for the exploits of Walter Hagen and Gene Sarazen.

Barnes was born in Lelant, England, in 1886. At age fifteen, he was made an assistant pro. He immigrated to San Francisco in 1906, and later became an American citizen. Still, he maintained close ties to his native country, playing in the British Open regularly and finishing in the top eight seven times between 1920 and 1928. The tallest of the champions of the first half of the century, Barnes won the first PGA Championship ever played, in 1916, and the next one, played in 1919.

Also in 1919, he produced the first book ever to use high-speed, frame-by-frame photography. His *Picture Analysis of Golf Strokes*, which became one of the most widely read instructional books of the era, featured full photographs of Barnes' strong, compact swing at various critical points. The book revolutionized printed golf instruction. Eighty years later it has become a prized possession of golf-book collectors.

Having won the 1921 U.S. Open at the Columbia Country Club by nine strokes, Barnes achieved one of the largest margins of victory of the twentieth century. In his U.S. Open victory, Barnes opened with a 69 to take a three-stroke lead and was never challenged. Barnes received the trophy from the hands of President Warren Harding, making him the first and only player in history to be given a U.S. Open trophy by the president of the United States.

Barnes had an angular, serious face that was topped by a mop of unruly hair. He was an intense, quiet competitor who often kept a sprig of clover or grass clenched tightly between his teeth. Barnes was one of the few players who wore trousers instead of knickers.

He didn't say much, but Barnes shared his wisdom when he felt the subject was worthy. He once told the young Bobby Jones, "You can't always be playing well when it counts. You'll never win golf tournaments until you learn how to score well when you're playing badly." The statement made a profound impact on Jones, who later wrote, "This is perhaps what I learned to do best of all."

Gene Sarazen rated him the finest five-iron player he had ever seen. In 1940, Barnes was chosen as one of the twelve original inductees into the PGA Hall of Fame.

The First Miniature Golf Course
Tourist Attraction

1927

BELOW: Garnet Carter's miniature golf course was certainly a tourist attraction in its day and a boon to his sagging hotel business.

OPPOSITE: A few society girls get their thrills playing on this odd course – there is no par – at the Hollywood Plaza Hotel in 1974.

Vacancies were up, and his hotel was losing money daily. Garnet Carter needed to do something to improve business. So when Carter built the first miniature golf course on Lookout Mountain, Tennessee, in 1927, he was not actually trying make history, but rather to publicize and bring in more traffic to his hotel and its full-length regulation golf course. To recoup some of his losses caused by the downturn in business at the hotel, Carter decided to charge a greens fee for using the miniature course as well.

Soon the miniature course became so popular, however, that more people wanted to play on it than on the regulation greens. To Carter's surprise, the course was overrun with adults, who liked the fantasy settings and relished the challenge of delicately negotiating a ball through mini-fairways.

Carter's little project was such a great success that the deluge of players actually trampled the miniature grounds into an unplayable state. Ever the opportunist, Carter secured rights to a vegetable fiber surface, and installed this for his patrons to play on. The advent of this durable surface encouraged a slew of entrepreneurs to open their own miniature golf courses, and soon they were popping up throughout the West into California, as well as in the Northeast.

Carter soon began manufacturing courses for national distribution under the name Tom Thumb Golf. A company called the Fairyland Manufacturing Company that produced gas station fixtures was contracted to manufacture the courses. By 1930, the business employed more than two hundred craftsmen for the various phases of prefabrication, which ranged from bending metal pipe for use as edging for the greens to hand decorating the little fountains, stairs, and other structures used as ornaments and obstacles. By the end of 1930, more than 25 million people were enthusiastic miniature golfers.

Even though the course closed in the mid1950s (the city decided to build a road through the area), the mini-golf business never looked back. Among its innovations were "swap-shops," where operators meet to exchange obstacles and hazards each year to keep their courses full of new surprises.

The First Graphite Shaft
Shakespeare Sporting Goods

COLUMBIA, SOUTH CAROLINA

1969

OPPOSITE: John Daly, who is long off the tee, was one of the first golfers to employ a graphite shaft.

BELOW: Ernie Els tees off on the first hole during the final round of the 2000 Masters at Augusta National Golf Course in Augusta, Georgia. He says that the graphite driver gives him extra distance and allows him "to attack the hole with better results."

Henry Shakespeare was certain that there was a way to do it. So Shakespeare, chairman of Shakespeare Sporting Goods, commissioned engineer Frank Thomas to create "the best golf shaft that could possibly be made."

Before he tapped Thomas' talents, Shakespeare's company had been involved in the production of a variety of sports equipment that used fiberglass composites. Among those products was a fiberglass golf shaft introduced in 1964. The golf shaft was not successful.

The company developed the process of filament winding on a metal bar known as a mandrel, in which strands of graphite are woven together form a composite material. When Union Carbide, producer of graphite fibers used in the space industry, suggested using them in a golf shaft, the modern graphite shaft was born. It was actually introduced in January 1970 at the PGA Merchandise Show in Orlando, Florida.

Graphite shafts are approximately thirty-four percent lighter than steel shafts; that lightness allows the golfer to develop more club head speed with less effort, making shots go farther. Some of today's tour pros prefer graphite to steel when they are teeing off.

"For club head speed, graphite shafts are a little lighter. If players want more club head speed, they will switch to graphite," Ernie Els notes. "I have steel shafts in all my clubs except the driver."

Despite the advantages of graphite, which were apparent even thirty years ago, it looked like fiberglass. So there was some skepticism about whether it would take off. Additionally, those first shafts cost $25 to produce, compared with only about $1.50 for steel shafts.

According to Thomas, some of the less expensive competition also lacked quality and gave graphite a bad name. "The cheaper shafts that came on the market delayed the wholesale conversion from steel to graphite," he said.

Many people think the development of effective graphite shafts has been a factor in changing the way the game is played. Watching some of the blasts Tiger and Els have had off the tee makes one wonder.

The First Father-and-Son Duo to Win on the Same Day

Bob and David Duval

1999

BELOW: Bob Duval of Neptune Beach, Florida, blasts out of a sand trap on the 12th during the first round of the Senior PGA's Vantage Championship at Tanglewood Park in Clemmons, North Carolina, in October 1999.

OPPOSITE: David Duval holds his trophy aloft after capturing The Players Championship (TPC) at Sawgrass in Ponte Vedra Beach, Florida, in 1999.

Like father, like son — both champions.

Sitting in a wooden folding chair, an hour after capturing his first Senior Tour victory, tears trickled down Bob Duval's cheeks as he watched his son David Duval accept the Players Championship crystal on March 27, 1999.

On a day when the PGA Tour crowned father-and-son champions for the first time, it was Bob who rang in with the first victory. Battling a stiff wind and a fierce charge by Bruce Fleisher, Duval made his final-round 1-over 71 stand up for a two-shot victory at the Emerald Coast Classic.

"I was really happy for myself and for my wife Shari, but for [David] to win that, it means so much to him," Bob Duval said. "To put your name on that [champion's] plaque, it's there forever. He made history again. And we made history."

The venues for these victories couldn't have been more appropriate. David is a native of nearby Jacksonville and grew up around The Players Championship at Sawgrass. A graduate of Florida State University in Tallahassee, Bob Duval has always held the Emerald Coast Classic close to his heart.

He received an exemption for the tournament in 1997, his first season on the senior tour. A third-place finish there allowed him to keep his card and turn the tour into a career, which he has parlayed into more than $1.5 million in earnings over three seasons. He has since let go of the teaching jobs he had held for years up and down the coast of North Florida.

Over the years, the elder Duval has seen his son come to the tournament and hang around the driving range, follow the players down number eighteen, and hope that one day he would hold that trophy in victory.

"The hardest place to win is at home," Bob Duval said. "Every time he tees it up there, he wants to win."

As for himself, Bob doesn't begrudge the fact it took him a long time to reach the enviable position he is in now. His focus is on building on what he has already accomplished. "I'm not looking back," Duval said of his late entry into the touring ranks. "I had great club jobs and everything else. I can't look back

at that. I'm playing probably better than I did then. And I couldn't win on the regular tour right now because those guys are too good."

With the victory worth a career-best at $165,000, Duval became this season's fourth first-time winner; and the fourth wire-to-wire winner that season.

For the second year in a row, they set an outstanding record for most combined earnings by a father-son team in the history of the PGA and Senior PGA Tours. Their grand total was $4,368,580, with David winning $3,641,906 by placing second on the PGA Tour.

CHAPTER 2

The Players

efore the endorsements, hefty purses, and eighteen majors won before the age of forty-six, Jack Nicklaus, the "Golden Bear," started off like everyone else — as an amateur.

"I think it's the spirit of amateur golf — and to play for the game itself and to play it with integrity — that's never left me. I would have been out of the game much sooner if it had," said Nicklaus, who won U.S. Amateur Championships in 1959 and 1961. "I still love to compete, to test myself, to play the game. That is the real lesson of champions like Bob Jones, and it's stayed deep inside."

Nicklaus was referring to Bobby Jones, the first amateur player to win a major. Jones held onto his amateur status even after he won the pre-modern "Grand Slam" in 1930, which included the British and U.S. Amateur Championships (see "The First Golfer to Win the Grand Slam," page 56).

Until the middle of the twentieth century, many of the world's best golfers held amateur status throughout their careers. They did it not only out of respect for the sport, but as a way to preserve their image in the eyes of their peers, fans, and the golfing administration, which collectively looked down on professional sportsmen.

Golf pros, from course designers to instructors, were employees at exclusive golf clubs who taught wealthy amateurs the finer points of the game. As such, they were generally considered of lesser social status, and not even allowed to use the clubhouse facilities. Naturally, these pioneering professionals wanted to play, too, and if not earn fame and fortune, then at least gain the respect they deserved.

Walter Hagen, a contemporary of Jones, was one of the first pros to insist on better treatment. Hagen's temperament was more suited to pure competitiveness, and he was never shy. Hagen was one of the sports' first true celebrities, a player who drew a new group of fans to the game, improved the status of his fellow pros, and helped build golf into a worldwide attraction (see "Golf's First Showman," page 58). With no fewer than eleven majors, he also left a record that remained unbroken until Nicklaus himself beat it.

While Jones, and Hagen's approaches and personalities diverged rather dramatically, each brought something vital to the game that has enhanced it for every player that followed, from Nicklaus to Tiger Woods.

Discover more about these legends of golf, as well as some other influential men and women who laid the critical groundwork for today's game.

OPPOSITE: American golfers Jack Nicklaus (left), Sam Snead (center), and Arnold Palmer get together at the first tee at Troon, Ayrshire, in Scotland in 1962. The three golfers were practicing for the British Open Golf Championship.

The First Golfer
to Lose Her Head

Mary, Queen of Scots

December 8, 1542-February 8, 1587

OPPOSITE: Queen Mary enjoys her favorite pastime with Chastelard (left), a young French courtier who often accompanied her, at St. Andrews Old Course in 1563.

BELOW: Mary, Queen of Scots was the first woman to practice golf in Scotland.

Her husband had been murdered and only recently laid to rest, but Mary Stuart just could not resist the urge to get out on the links.

Some might even argue that Mary's passion for golf — plus the political threat she posed to her cousin Elizabeth I, of course — contributed to her demise. Mary was spotted playing a few rounds of golf at St. Andrews shortly after the death by strangulation of her husband, Lord Darnley, in 1567. Though Darnley had not been innocent, having both betrayed and plotted against Mary from the early days of their marriage, her seeming callousness in response to his death aroused the disapproval of her people. She lost their favor permanently when she not only refused to prosecute the man suspected of the murder, the Earl of Bothwell, but actually married him. Without popular support, Mary was forced to throw herself at Elizabeth's mercy.

Mary came by her love of golf honestly, as she was by no means the first royal to enjoy the game. In 1502, after a truce with the English had reduced the need for archery practice, James IV of Scotland (Mary's grandfather) lifted the ban on golf. He then commissioned a set of clubs for himself, appointing the craftsman his royal clubmaker. Mary's own son, James I of England, was also known as an avid golfer; he passed on the passion to his two sons as well.

Mary's own contribution to the game goes beyond being one of the first female players on record. In fact, Mary is given credit for introducing the caddy to the game of golf. The story goes that when Mary went to France as a young girl, King Louis learned that she was passionate about golf. So, to accommodate her affinity, he had the very first golf course outside of Scotland built for her enjoyment. To make sure that she was properly looked after while she played he ordered cadets from a military school to accompany her. Mary took such a liking to being assisted on her golf outings that when she returned to Scotland she took the practice with her. In French the word cadet is pronounced "ca-day" and it was later anglicized to caddy.

Upon fleeing Scotland in 1568, Mary was tried for her role in the killing of Darnley, and remained a prisoner of the government of England for the rest of her life. Bothwell died in a Danish prison. Though Elizabeth was not a strict jailer, Mary plotted ceaselessly to regain her freedom and even to claim the English throne. Finally, in 1587, she was beheaded.

The First Golfer to Win the "Grand Slam"

Bobby Jones

March 17, 1902 – December 18, 1971

1930

CAREER HIGHLIGHTS
U.S. Open: 1923, 1926, 1929, 1930; U.S. Amateur: 1924, 1925, 1927, 1928, 1930; British Open: 1926, 1927, 1930; British Amateur: 1930

USPGA Hall Of Fame: 1940
World Golf Hall of Fame: 1974

ABOVE: Bobby Jones holds the trophy after capturing the British Open Championship in 1927, his second consecutive triumph there.

OPPOSITE: Bobby Jones drives from the fairway during the 1930 British Open Golf Tournament.

Before Tiger Woods took his recent "Grand Slam," there was another star: Mr. Bobby Jones.

Between 1926 and 1930, no one had a more stellar major championship record than Bobby Jones. Despite his amateur status, Jones was an awesome champion.

A native of Atlanta, Georgia, Jones played in four British Opens, winning three of them; he also won four U.S. Opens. And in the total of twelve U.S. and British Opens in which Jones played from 1922 to 1930, he only once finished lower than second place. Jones is best remembered, however, for accomplishing what used to be considered the Grand Slam. In 1930, he won the British Amateur Championship, the British Open, the U.S. Open, and the U.S. Amateur Championship, in that order.

Nowadays, being an amateur champion is considered a jumping-off point before turning professional. Yet, back in the 1920s and '30s, many of the world's best players held amateur status throughout their golfing careers. Jones was the model amateur not purely because of his world-class record, but also because of the way in which he upheld the spirit of amateurism. He would neither bow to the pressures of commercialism nor profit from the results of his achievements. To do so, he believed, would have clearly violated his status as an amateur.

Jones' career began in earnest when, at the age of fourteen, he entered his first national championship, the 1916 National Amateur, at the Merion Cricket Club near Philadelphia. He lost, and the championships were suspended until the end of World War I. During that period, he played matches to earn money for war relief funds. In 1920, he entered his first U.S. Open. In 1923, at Inwood, he won his first U.S. Open. Coming into the final hole even with Bobby Cruickshank, he hit a shot so legendary that the members of Inwood marked the spot with a plaque. It was the beginning of an incredible series of victories.

One of the classic moments in Jones' remarkable tenure and in British Open history occurred in 1926 in a match at Royal Lytham and St. Annes. He and Al Watrous arrived even at the seventeenth. Watrous landed his drive perfectly, but Jones ended up in a shallow bunker to the left of the seventeenth fairway and 170 yards (153m) from the green. From there Jones lofted a sweet shot to within twelve feet (3.6m) of the cup. Watrous three-putted, but Jones did it in two. From a seemingly certain bogey on the hole's par-4, Jones snatched victory to save par and secure the win. No American had ever before won a British Open at Royal Lytham. He went on to become the first person to win the British and U.S. Opens in one year.

After completing the Grand Slam in 1930, Bobby Jones retired from tournament golf. He was only twenty-eight. His short yet stunningly successful golf career gave way to a thriving professional life in law—not that Jones dismissed golf altogether.

Along with financier Clifford Roberts, Bobby Jones founded the Augusta National Golf Club in Atlanta, Georgia. He wanted to create a course that reflected his ideas about design; he chose as a site an old indigo plantation, and as architect, Dr. Alister Mackenzie of Scotland, who held similar ideas about course design. Augusta opened officially in 1933. Jones wanted more than just a course of his own; he also wanted to host an invitational tournament — which is how Augusta National became the home of the Masters Tournament. The first Masters was played in 1934; Jones came in thirteenth. He continued to play recreationally, and occasionally in the Masters, until 1948. He also wrote books and made a number of instructional films on golf. In 1950 Jones was diagnosed with a rare degenerative disease, and spent the rest of his life in poor health.

Clean-cut, charming, and courteous, Bobby Jones went unassumingly about his business on the golf course and off. Though he was known for the occasional show of ill temper, Jones was the antithesis of such showy characters as Walter Hagen and Gene Sarazen. Gracious in victory and defeat, he was, and remains, a hero of the game.

Today, Bobby Jones' famous putter, "Calamity Jane," is on display at Augusta National. The putter was almost lost in 1925, when a fire at the Eastlake Golf Club claimed the rest of Jones's clubs — Calamity Jane, however, was safe at home under Bobby's bed.

Golf's First Showman
Walter Hagen

December 21, 1892-October 5, 1969

CAREER HIGHLIGHTS
U.S. Open: 1914, 1919;
USPGA: 1921, 1924, 1925,
1926, 1927; British Open:
1922, 1924, 1928, 1929;
Ryder Cup: 1927-35, 1937

USPGA Hall Of Fame: 1940
World Golf Hall of Fame:
1974

BELOW: Golf's first
showman flashes a winning
smile while posing for the
camera after capturing the
British Open in 1928.

OPPOSITE: Walter Hagen
works out of the rough
during a match between the
United States and England
in 1930.

f *Gentleman's Quarterly* put out an issue featuring the most stylish golfers in history, Walter Hagen would undoubtedly top the list. His natty duds — Hagen made wearing knickers fashionable and was known for his white flannel trousers — and self-assured manner on the golf course and off helped this poor boy from Rochester, New York, to make a lasting impact on golf as both a player and showman.

On the cover of his autobiography, *The Walter Hagen Story*, he is quoted as saying: "I never wanted to be a millionaire… I just wanted to live like one." And that he did.

As golf's first flamboyant character, Hagen was known for his glamorous lifestyle — being chauffeured about in his limousine, enjoying his Scotch into the bleary-eyed hours of the morning — even during tournaments. Despite these glitzy ways, Hagen was an unflappable competitor, especially during matchplay. He was also golf's first full-time professional player.

In a career that spanned more than twenty years, Walter Hagen collected eleven professional major titles. At his peak, between 1913 and 1930, the U.S. Masters didn't exist, and though he also lost a couple of years of competition to the First World War his record was still outstanding.

Despite being one of golf's all-time greats, Hagen was never particularly good off the tee. However, he handily made up for that shortcoming with his impressive short game. While Hagen's errant drives often cost him — he would drive the ball off the fairway on a regular basis — his approaches, as well as his putting, were masterful. He once noted, "I expect to make at least seven mistakes a round. Therefore, when I make a bad shot, it's just one of the seven."

Hagen won two U.S. Opens and four British Opens, but where he really excelled was in matchplay. He won five USPGA

Championships, including four consecutive matches beginning in 1924. He also had a good Ryder Cup record, winning seven of his nine contests and losing only once. In 1922, Hagen became the first American-born player to win the British Open.

Hagen gets the credit for raising the social status of professional golfers. In his day, professional golfers — as employees of the clubs — were held in lower social esteem than the wealthy members were. Hagen rejected that kind of snobbery, handling situations in his uniquely inimitable style. When Hagen first came to England to play in the 1920 British Open at Deal, professionals were not allowed to enter the clubhouse through the front door: they were required to use either a side or back entrance. Hagen shocked the game's establishment when he made a point

of not going into a clubhouse at all — instead, he parked his limousine in the club's driveway and had everything he needed, including champagne, delivered to the car. He refused to accept second-class treatment.

Hagen's clashes with the golf establishment on both sides of the Atlantic were legendary. Its entertainment value aside, his colorful personality not only helped to democratize the game, but also raised its profile in general. The result was an increase in sponsorship, which opened the doors to a new generation of talented players. And as Hagen's great rival, Gene Sarazen, once commented: "All the players who have a chance to go after big money should say a silent prayer to Walter Hagen. It was Walter who made professional golf what it is."

The First Player to Popularize the Overlapping Grip

Harry Vardon

May 9, 1870 – March 20, 1937

CAREER HIGHLIGHTS
British Open: 1896, 1898, 1899, 1903, 1911, 1914; U.S. Open: 1900; PGA Match-play: 1912

World Golf Hall of Fame: 1974

OPPOSITE: As the gallery watches intently, Harry Vardon drives from the fairway en route to a win over two American professionals at Fox Hills Golf Club on Staten Island in 1920.

BELOW: The first to grip the golfing public on the way to hold a club, Harry Vardon, winner of a record six British Opens, was a true pioneer of the game.

Harry Vardon wasn't the first to actually do it, but he was the one who made it famous.

Though Johnny Laidlay was the first to use the overlapping grip in golf, it was Vardon who gave the technique its renown. The "Vardon Grip," in which the pinky finger of the right hand overlaps the index finger of the left in the right-handed grip, is still widely used among today's golfers, and serves as an effective alternative to the interlocking grip or the baseball grip.

The Vardon Grip, according to golf professionals, is well-suited to golfers with large hands. It's no coincidence that Vardon had enormous ones, which fit perfectly around a club. Despite his big mitts, Vardon was not a large man, standing just 5 feet, 9 inches (172.5cm) tall and weighing 155 pounds (70kg).

Vardon was born in the Channel Islands in England, one of eight children. Known for his generous, even temperament, at the age of thirteen, Vardon decided to follow in his father's footsteps and become a gardener.

When a golf course was to be built in town, Vardon and several of his siblings created one of their own. It was there that Vardon repeatedly and diligently practiced the upright swing that would one day help him become a champion. As a youth, however, he played very few actual rounds of golf, and indeed, never had a formal lesson. Vardon played in a few tournaments in his late teens, and didn't decide to make golf a career until he saw his older brother, Tom, who had turned professional, do well in tournaments.

Vardon won the British Open six times, a record that still holds today. He, James Braid, and J.H. Taylor, also innovators of the game, were called the "Triumvirate" because of their domination of the sport in the early twentieth century. After Vardon's 1903 British Open win, he was diagnosed with tuberculosis. He came back to win again in 1911 and 1914, taking the latter victory at the age of forty-four.

Vardon's distinctive swing was more upright than that of other players of his era. His balls tended to fly higher and longer, and he was more accurate off the tee than most. He also made it look easy — at Vardon's funeral, J. H. Taylor remembered, "He got his effects with that delightful, effortless ease that was tantalizing." The legend was that his shots always flew straight down the fairway, and Taylor agreed, noting that Vardon "played fewer shots out of the rough than anyone who has ever swung a golf club."

Although Vardon played in constrictive attire — he wore knickers, a collared shirt and tie, and tightly buttoned jacket — his effortless swing wasn't hindered one bit. The way in which he deftly and efficiently attacked his shots, sweeping the club under the ball so as to leave a little divot, has been the standard by which all golfers who have followed him have been measured.

"Relaxation," he said, "added to a few necessary fundamental principles, is the basis of this great game."

The First American to Win the British Ladies' Amateur

Babe Zaharias

June 26, 1914 – September 27, 1956

1947

CAREER HIGHLIGHTS
Western Open: 1940, 1944,
1945, 1950; U.S. Women's
Amateur: 1946; British
Ladies' Amateur: 1947;
Titleholders Championship:
1947, 1950, 1952; U.S.
Women's Open: 1945,
1950, 1954

Leading Money Winner:
1950-51
Vare Trophy: 1954
LPGA Hall of Fame: 1951
Bob Jones Award: 1957
World Golf Hall of Fame:
1974
USPGA Hall of Fame: 1976

BELOW: Before she
became a professional golfer,
Mildred "Babe" Zaharias
was a world-class Olympian.

OPPOSITE: The Babe
and her husband, George,
celebrate aboard the Queen
Elizabeth after winning the
British Ladies' Amateur.

Natural talent is really something to marvel at, especially when it is sharpened by practice and displayed at the highest level of competition. Athletes who can apply those innate gifts not to just one sport, but to several — and excel at all of them — are truly riveting. They are also very rare.

Mildred (Babe) Didrikson Zaharias was one of those athletes, a woman who carved out an important niche in several sports, particularly golf.

She originally made a living working for the Casualty Insurance Company while playing both basketball and baseball for the company teams. (She took the nickname "Babe" after hitting five home runs in one game.) She then entered eight events in the 1932 National Track and Field Championships and won six of them, setting four world records in the process. Babe went on to win two gold medals (javelin and eighty-meter hurdles) and one silver (high jump) in the 1932 Olympic Games in Los Angeles. Zaharias might have taken gold in all three events but she was disqualified in high jump — after setting a new world record — for using the revolutionary "Western Roll" technique, which was judged "unladylike."

Still, these victories vaulted Zaharias onto the world stage. And it was also during those Olympic Games that the famous American sportswriter Grantland Rice suggested she try applying some of that athletic ability to the game of golf.

Not surprisingly, on the golf course Zaharias immediately showed the same knack for picking up a sport, as well as a truly remarkable power. (It has been said that at a course on the east coast of Scotland she once blasted her way onto the green at the 540-yard (486m) fifteenth with only a drive and a 4-iron.) She played her first tournament in 1934; just a year later she won the Texas Women's Amateur Championship.

The USGA immediately disqualified her from further amateur tournaments, and she played professionally until her amateur status was reinstated in 1943. In 1946-47 she won a string of seventeen consecutive tournaments — an unprecedented and still unequaled feat. Her victories included both the 1946 U.S. Women's Amateur and the 1947 British Ladies' Amateur, the latter a title that had eluded her great predecessor, Glenna Collett Vare, making Zaharias the first American ever to win this British title since its inception.

In 1947, Zaharias turned professional again and continued to dominate the sport. She became a founder and charter member of the LPGA. Zaharias was the leading money winner on the professional tour for four consecutive years starting in 1948; she won a total of thirty-one U.S. professional events in an illustrious career.

In 1951 she and Patty Berg went with a team of American women players to Britain to play a match against a team of scratch London amateurs, including the former English champion Leonard Crawley. Zaharias' team won all their singles, playing the men even. In the head-to-head match against Crawley, Zaharias took a pass on his offer to use "the ladies' tees," and went on to beat him.

In 1953, Zaharias underwent surgery for colon cancer. The next year, she won five more victories, including one of her greatest, the 1954 U.S. Women's Open. Her battle with cancer was not over, but she continued to play, winning twice in 1955. Even against Zaharias' incredible fortitude, however, ultimately the disease proved relentless, and she died on September 27, 1956, at the age of forty-two.

The First Golfer To Come Back From a Near-Fatal Injury

Ben Hogan

August 13, 1912 – July 25, 1997

1949

CAREER HIGHLIGHTS
U.S. Open: 1946, 1950,
1951, 1953; USPGA: 1946,
1948; U.S. Masters:
1951, 1953; British Open:
1953

Vardon Trophy: 1940,
1941, 1948
USPGA Player of the Year:
1948, 1950, 1951, 1953
USPGA Hall of Fame: 1953
World Golf Hall of Fame:
1974
Bob Jones Award: 1976

OPPOSITE: Ben Hogan
plays in the rain at Fort
Worth, Texas, in the
Masters Championship
at Augusta National Golf
Club on April 9, 1954.

His is an improbable story. The life of Ben Hogan was filled with tragedy and heartache and despite it all Hogan went on to become one of the greatest golfers ever to play the game.

Hogan's courage was tested in his early years away from the golf course. At the age of nine, his father committed suicide leaving Hogan's mother to single-handedly raise him and his two siblings. To help provide for the family Hogan sold newspapers and worked at odd jobs. It was through these times that he formed his steadfast determination, for which he was later known on the golf course.

Hogan first discovered golf as a fifteen-year-old caddy at Glen Garden Country Club in Fort Worth, Texas, where coincidentally, he lost the caddy championship in a playoff to another boy his age named Byron Nelson.

He turned professional at seventeen and joined the tour full-time as a nineteen-year-old in 1931. By the age of thirty-three he was the world's top player, earning nicknames like "Bantam Ben" and "the Hulk" for his compact build, stoic nature, and fierce game.

Initially, although he had success in several tournaments, his game wasn't strong enough to make him competitive in the majors. But Hogan's determination prevailed and he worked hard to fine-tune his game. He would sometimes even show up two days prior to a tournament and study the course. Ever the perfectionist, he kept his eyes solely focused on the greens, which meant that he never played to the gallery. As a result, throughout the years Hogan was always well respected, but never especially liked.

By 1940, Hogan had become the leading money earner on the U.S. Tour. However, the war interrupted his career and it was not until 1946, at the age of thirty-four that Hogan won his first major. He made his Ryder Cup debut the following year. And just as Hogan's career began to soar, he had a near-fatal car accident in 1949.

In February of that year, in the countryside outside Van Horn, Texas, about 150 miles (241.4km) east of El Paso, Hogan's car was demolished when a Greyhound bus met Hogan's car head on. While his wife, Valerie, sustained only minor injuries, Hogan suffered a broken collarbone, a smashed rib, a double fracture of the pelvis, and a broken ankle. After his bones were set in an El Paso hospital, it appeared Hogan would make a good recovery. Soon after, however, he developed a blood clot, and doctors performed an operation to tie off the principal veins in his legs, preventing the clot from reaching his heart.

There was doubt as to whether he would be able to walk again, let alone play golf. Hogan's resolve carried him through and he returned to competitive golf a year later. In memory of his plight, the Ben Hogan award is given annually to a golfer who has successfully recovered from injury to compete again.

Hogan's return to competitive golf after the devastating accident that nearly ended his career and his life was a miraculous feat. But then consider that in his first tournament after the accident, less than a year after having been told that he may never walk again, Hogan tied Sam Snead for first place before losing in a playoff. Hogan was back, and seemingly more determined than ever.

Although he had to scale back his appearances on the tour due to lingering leg pain, Hogan decided to concentrate mainly on

BELOW: Ben Hogan glares at the photographer as he waits for his second shot in the Los Angeles Open Golf tournament on First Fairway in Los Angeles, California, in January 1950. This is Hogan's first competitive appearance since his accident. The sign in the background asks that photographers not bother Hogan.

OPPOSITE: Ben Hogan, one of the nation's leading golfers, and his wife, Valerie, at a hospital in El Paso, Texas, in February 1949.

the majors, and in 1950, only sixteen months after the accident, he won his second U.S. Open title at Merion, outside Philadelphia. After two rounds, he was two shots back behind leader Dutch Harrison. Hogan managed to literally limp his way through the final thirty-six holes and into a three-way tie at 287 with Lloyd Mangrum and George Fazio with the help of his now famous one-iron shot on the 18th. In the playoff, Hogan left them in the dust, shooting a 69 to their 73s. It was truly an amazing comeback. It didn't end there. Hogan went on to win the U.S Open again in 1951. In that same year he also won his first Masters with a then-record 274. In 1953, at the age of forty-one, Hogan played in only six tournaments. He won five of them. Three of them were majors — his fourth U.S. Open, his second Masters, and he won the British Open in his only appearance ever in that tournament. All told, Hogan won six majors after his accident.

Hogan's career numbers include sixty-three victories (second only to Sam Snead's eighty-one and Jack Nicklaus' seventy), nine major championships, and four U.S. Open titles. He died at the age of eighty-four in 1997 after a long battle with Alzheimer's.

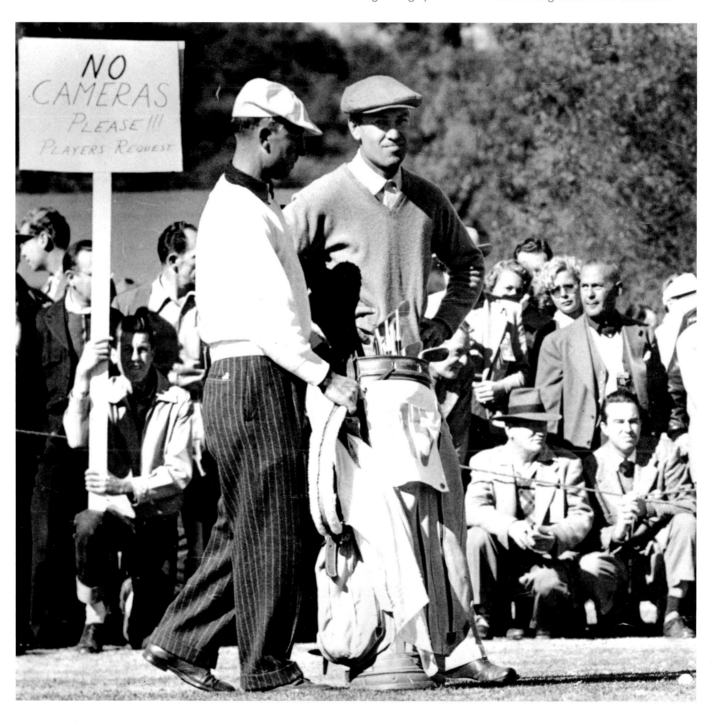

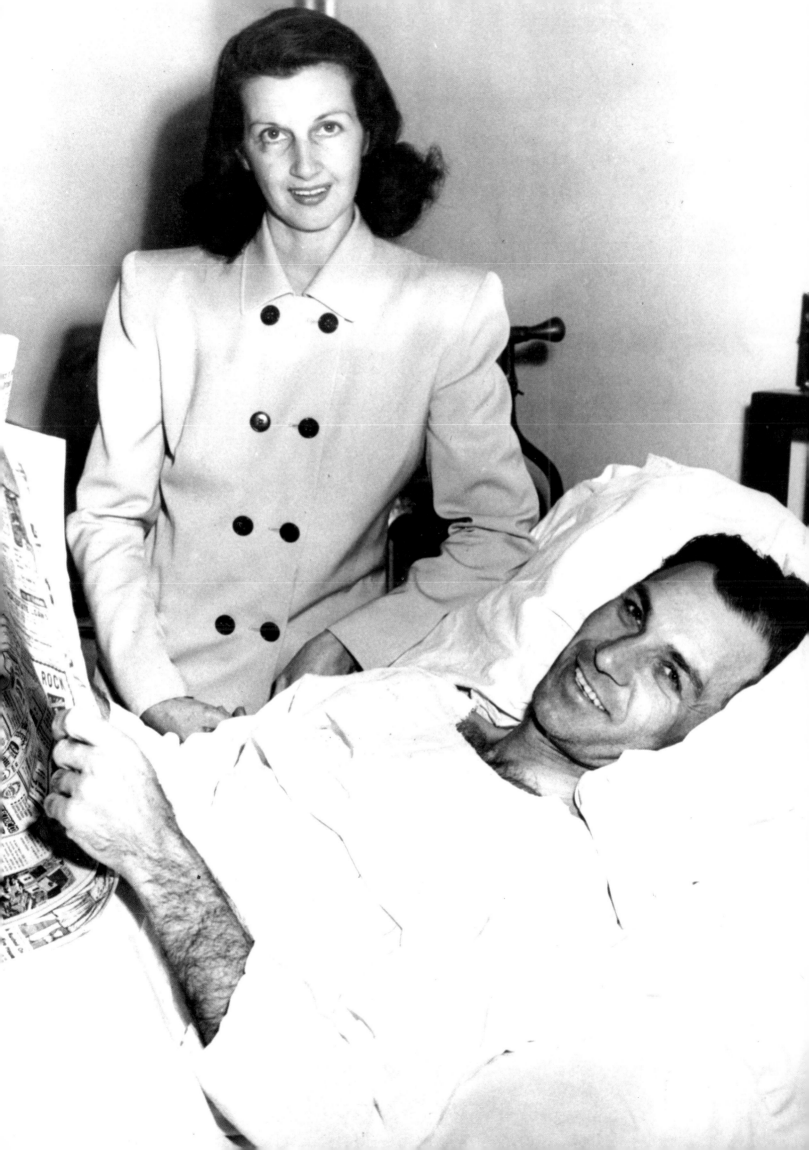

First Player to Shoot his Age
Sam Snead

May 27, 1927– May 23, 2002

1979

CAREER HIGHLIGHTS
USPGA: 1942, 1949, 1951;
British Open: 1946; U.S.
Masters: 1949, 1952, 1954;
USPGA Seniors: 1964,
1965, 1967, 1970, 1972,
1973; World Seniors: 1964,
1965, 1970, 1972, 1973;
Winner of 81 U.S. Tour
Events: 1936-65

Vardon Trophy: 1938, 1949-
50, 1955
USPGA Player of the Year:
1949
USPGA Hall of Fame: 1953
World Golf Hall of Fame:
1974

RIGHT: Sam Snead
takes a break from golf as
he unhooks a 1 1/2 pound
bass he caught while fishing
in a small pond on the
course of Augusta, Georgia,
after practice in April 1973.

OPPOSITE: Slammin'
Sam Snead, nicknamed for
going long off the tee, drives
down the fairway during
the first round of the 1941
Masters.

Slammin' Sam Snead, whose remarkable career includes a whopping record eighty-one PGA events from 1936 to 1965, was the youngest player to score his age (and below) in a PGA Tour event when, at the age of sixty-seven, he shot a 67 and 66 at the 1979 Quad Cities Open. Thirty years earlier, he had inaugurated the green jacket tradition at Augusta, as the first winner to be awarded the now famous sport coat.

The youngest of five, Snead grew up in Ashwood, Virginia, a place that boasted more amateur whiskey distillers than professional golf instructors. He learned to golf from watching his oldest brother, Homer, whose booming drives across the fields on their cow and chicken farm inspired Sam to try his hand at the game. (His first love had been football, but an injury ended those dreams.) From whacking balls in the back-woods as a youngster to nailing beauties on the back nine as a caddy playing with the big boys near his hometown, Snead's game progressed to a point where it became inevitable he would go pro.

Snead went to California for the start of the 1937 season, and in just his third event won the Oakland Open with four sub-par rounds, for a total of 270. He won five more times that year and, incredibly, was the runner-up for the season's U.S. Open. If there was one event that Snead would have loved to do over, it was the 1939 U.S. Open. With only three years of professional golf to his credit, the then twenty-seven-year-old was hoping to establish himself as one of the game's brightest lights by winning the major. Making a simple par five on the 558-yard (502m) eighteenth hole at the Philadelphia Country Club would have clinched the title for him.

Snead made eight. He hooked his drive into the trampled rough, then took a brassie (a two-and-a-half wood) and knocked the ball into a bunker about 110 yards (99m) short of the green. Trying to get on in three, he played an eight-iron and left it in the bunker. He swung again and dumped the ball into yet another bunker just short of the green. He finally made it on in five, but he was still forty-five feet (13.5m) from the pin. He three-putted. In a matter of minutes, his great victory had become a horrifying defeat. A U.S. Open victory continued to elude him, although he finished second three more times.

Snead later explained how he mistakenly thought he needed a birdie to win, and he confessed to the number-one sin in golf. "In all honesty," he wrote, "I have to admit that I was guilty of bad thinking."

Lapses in judgment, as well as in play, weren't the norm for Snead. He holds the Masters record for most consecutive finishes with twenty-four. At the age of sixty-two, after racking up a remarkable slew of victories and awards, Snead was still competitive when most others his age were on the wane. He finished in third place in the USPGA Championship in 1974, behind Lee Trevino and Jack Nicklaus, and ahead of Gary Player; a few months before, he had been runner-up in the Los Angeles Open. At the age of seventy-one, he won a PGA Club Professionals title, and has taken some fourteen Senior Tour victories.

Snead, whose nickname came from his long drives, molded his game into a model of efficiency and elegance. His country boy persona was shaped with the help of promoter Fred Corcoran, who rarely missed an opportunity to play up Snead's "hillbilly" background, and once even coaxed Snead into playing barefoot. After American idol Bobby Jones left the stage, the golfing public craved someone to replace him as the next hero of the sport. Snead, over the course of a memorable career, made the role of golf hero his own. Snead died in May of 2002 at the age of eighty-nine after a prolonged illness.

The First African-American to Qualify for the LPGA Tour

Althea Gibson

August 25, 1927 –

1963

OPPOSITE: Jackie Robinson (left) and Althea Gibson, two of the most gifted African-American athletes in the history of sport, compare scorecards after the second round of the ninth annual North-South Golf Tournament at the Miami Springs course in Miami, Florida, in 1962.

BELOW: Althea Gibson, shown here with her caddy, consults him on club choice before taking a shot.

Few people can claim to have advanced the cause of racial equality in one sport, but Althea Gibson did it in two. In golf and tennis, two arenas long dominated by the white establishment, the gritty and gifted Gibson beat the odds to become a winner, fighting to play during an era when segregation was still the norm.

Born in South Carolina, the daughter of sharecroppers, Gibson moved to New York City as a small child. Before she took to the links, Gibson's game was tennis. A New York Police Athletic League coach named Buddy Walker saw the girl playing paddleball in the tough streets of Harlem, and recognized her athletic ability. She finally agreed to join the coach at a nearby public court to try and learn tennis.

Gibson's talent was immediately apparent. Walker bought her a pair of second-hand wooden tennis racquets and taught her the basic rules of the game. In her first series of matches — playing against more experienced teenage boys — Gibson, already becoming an intimidating force, clobbered all comers.

From there, playing in the American Tennis Association, the nation's oldest African-American sports organization, she went on to capture six consecutive New York State championships. Beginning in 1944, Gibson was the ATA's number one player for seven straight years.

The logical next step was to begin competing in the all-white world of the United States Ladies Tennis Association (USLTA); however, Gibson was denied every time she tried to enter a tournament.

Finally, Alice Marble, a respected former U.S. Open champion who admired Gibson's talents, wrote a searing letter to the editor that was published in the July 1950 *American Lawn Tennis* magazine. In the letter, Marble wrote that she was embarrassed by "the bigotry" exhibited by her fellow members of the USLTA.

One week later, Gibson received an invitation to the following month's U.S. Open.

And on August 28, 1950, Gibson stepped onto Court 14 at Forest Hills and defeated Barbara Knapp 6-2, 6-2. It was the first U.S. Open match to include an African-American athlete.

Seven years later, in 1957, she became the first African-American to win Wimbledon. Later that year, she also captured the U.S. Women's Open title. Amazingly, the following year she duplicated that effort, successfully defending both major titles.

In 1960, a friend took her out for a casual round of golf, and Gibson caught the bug, eventually trading in her tennis racquet for golf clubs. It took Gibson only three years to acquire the requisite skills to become the first African-American to qualify for the LPGA Tour in 1963. Gibson competed on the LPGA Tour full-time throughout the racially charged 1960s.

The LPGA had a long-standing tradition of opposing exclusionary, bigoted policies. Acting commissioner Lenny Wirtz, supported by the LPGA membership, officially instituted an "all play" or "all stay away" rule, which meant that unless all the tour members were welcome at a particular club or tournament, none would play there. Sadly, that policy was tested a few times during the decade, but the LPGA was always able to find sponsors for whom race was unimportant.

Although Gibson's golf career did not include any major tournament victories, her courage and persistence make her an integral part of the history and heritage of the LPGA. Althea's pioneering efforts paved the way for such gifted athletes as Venus Williams and Tiger Woods.

The First Australian to Win a Major

Peter Thomson

May 27, 1927 –

1954

CAREER HIGHLIGHTS

New Zealand Open:
1950-51, 1953, 1955, 1959-61, 1965, 1971; Australian
Open: 1951, 1967, 1972;
British Open: 1954-56,
1958, 1965

PGA Matchplay: 1954, 1961,
1966-67
British Masters: 1961, 1968
USPGA Seniors: 1984;
British PGA Seniors: 1988
World Golf Hall of Fame:
1988
Honorary Member of the
Royal & Ancient Golf Club

RIGHT: Australia's Peter
Thomson plays from the
edge of the bunker on the
fifth green at the 1958
British Open Championship
at St. Annes On-The-Sea
in England.

OPPOSITE:
Peter Thomson holds
the trophy he received for
winning his fourth British
Open Golf Championship
at Royal Lytham and
St. Annes in Lancashire
England on July 5, 1958.
He beat Dave Thomas of
Wales by four strokes in
a 36-hole playoff.

Revered as the father of Australian golf and one of the world's leading golfers during the 1950s, Peter Thomson's professional golfing career was originally a secondary pursuit — his intended profession was industrial chemistry.

One of four boys, Thomson began playing golf at the age of twelve at the Royal Park course in the working-class suburb of Brunswick in Melbourne. His natural talent was soon obvious, and within three years he was champion of his local club.

After winning the prestigious Victorian Amateur Championship, the twenty-year-old Thomson decided to turn professional. He played his first British Open in 1951, coming in sixth. In 1954 he won the event, and therefore his first Major, at Royal Lytham and St. Annes. One of the classic moments in that year's tournament came when Thomson, after a splendid drive at the par-5 sixteenth, slightly miscued his fairway wood second shot, leaving his ball in a bunker about 25 yards (22.5m) from the pin. From this potentially difficult situation, the twenty-four-year-old Aussie exploded to within two feet (60cm) of the flag and nailed the putt. Thomson went on to win by one stroke.

It was the first of five British Open victories for Thomson, including three successive championships in 1954, 1955, and 1956. Another memorable victory came in 1965, when he beat the terrific troika of Palmer, Nicklaus, and Player. In playing twenty-one Opens, Thomson placed second three times, and finished in the top ten no fewer than seventeen times. Harry Vardon, with six British Opens to his credit, is the only player with more.

Thomson rarely played North American courses, and became famous for promoting golf primarily in Australia, where he was president of the PGA. Despite his dislike of American courses, Thomson joined the PGA Senior Tour in 1985, and won nine of twenty-seven tournaments on the circuit, earning over $1 million in prize money.

Later in his career, he became a course designer, golf writer, and television commentator. He was also a popular speaker on many subjects. Known as the ambassador of golf in Australia and Asia, Thomson has been instrumental in establishing the reputation and prestige that golf tournaments there now enjoy.

ON. W. J. 79 69–148
KEMP
.H. 70 71 72
KING.
K. J. 85
KNIGH
70
LARC
(A) 76
ARC
(A) 7
ST
.M. 7
-ASS

The First African-American Golfer to Win a National Championship
Bill Wright

April 4, 1936 –

1959

BELOW: A proud Bill Wright holds up the winning trophy with USGA Commissioner Joseph C. Dey after securing the 1959 US Amateur Public Links Championship.

While the USGA has had a long-standing policy of preserving unblemished amateurism, for a significant period it either scoffed at those amateurs who were African-American, or refused to let them compete in sanctioned events.

Efforts to exclude certain categories of players are part of the history of golf, but so are attempts to integrate the game. In 1896, at the U.S. Open at Shinnecock Hills, John Shippen, an African-American whose father was a minister to the Shinnecock Indians, and Oscar Bunn, a member of the Shinnecock tribe, both played over the protests of at least some of the golf professionals, most of whom were transplanted Scotsmen.

USGA president Theodore Havemeyer didn't bat an eye. "We will play the Open with you," he said to the grumbling professionals, "or without you."

Shippen, who finished fifth among twenty-eight competitors, played in five more U.S. Opens, the last in 1913, and is recognized today as the first native-born American professional golfer. Still, bigotry remained. In 1938, the USGA refused to accept an Open entry from an African-American golfer. And when the Miami Country Club notified the USGA "that it would not permit Negroes to compete in the 1952 Amateur Public Links championship on its course," the USGA, unwilling to infringe on what it regarded as the prerogative of a member club, failed to fight the decision.

As the United States' cultural landscape and attitudes began to shift and society became less bigoted, the USGA began to reflect, albeit slowly and often reluctantly, the changes that were taking place. Policies that had formerly been very rigid loosened considerably to allow African-American players real access at last.

William Wright was one of the first.

Breaking par may have been of more interest to him than breaking the color barrier, but for Wright, one followed upon the other.

A 1956 graduate of Seattle's Franklin High School, Wright came to Western College in Los Angeles to play basketball. But his real passion was golf, and he played both sports for the school's Vikings.

As a junior in 1959, he won the U.S. Amateur Public Links Championship, becoming the first African-American to win a USGA title. One year later, he won the National Association of Intercollegiate Athletics golf tourney, the first individual NAIA championship in Western's history.

He was, as USGA *Golf Journal* reported, "a legend despite his time."

Forty years later, Wright remains a champion. In 1968, when Western established its Athletic Hall of Fame, Wright was one of the first seven inductees.

Now, once a year, he takes time off from his job as a teaching professional at The Lakes at El Segunda, near Los Angeles International Airport, to return to Western to support the Alumni Golf Classic, named in his honor. And while he's "in the neighborhood," he stops off in Seattle to give tips on golf, and life, to young people who look to him as a trailblazer and role model.

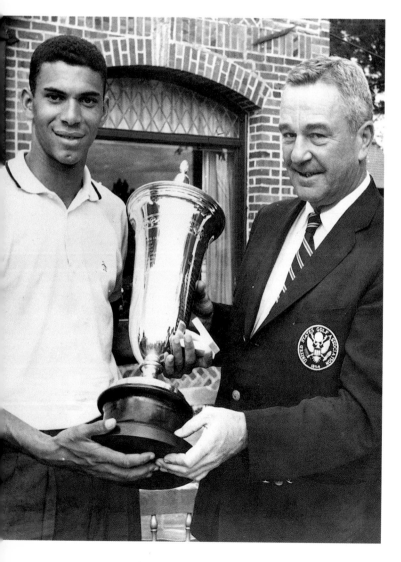

The First Golfer to Order a Pizza During a U.S. Open

Lori Garbacz

August 11, 1958 –

1958

ABOVE: Lori Garbacz watches where her ball goes after striking it during a LPGA tournament.

She couldn't wait any longer. The molasses-slow pace between shots and groupings begged for something to be done.

When she had to wait an excruciating forty-five minutes on the fourth tee at the 1991 Open at Colonial Country Club in Fort Worth, Lori Garbacz, a long-time golf-pro and sporadic player on the LPGA Tour, knew she and her group were about to log some serious hours.

By the time Garbacz reached the fourteenth hole, she was so fed up that she had to take action. She spotted a bank of pay phones and sent her caddy over to order a pizza from a nearby Domino's, since it was abundantly clear she was going to be on the course well past suppertime.

She gave instructions to her caddy to tell the deliveryman that in forty-five minutes, he should be able to find us on the seventeenth tee. And true to Domino's guarantee that they will deliver in 30 minute or less, there was a scalding hot large cheese pie waiting for Garbacz and her group.

The slow play, Garbacz contended, should be blamed on the players, not the USGA. She likened playing in the Open, (one of her better days at the tournament was in 1984 when she tied for third) to driving to the Hamptons for the weekend and finding yourself in snarled in traffic on the Long Island Expressway.

In almost two decades on the Tour, Garbacz has the same number of victories as she does for pizza deliveries: one. Her only win came at the 1989 Circle K LPGA Tucson Open.

The First Man to Hit a Golf Ball in Space

Alan Shepard

November 18, 1923 – August 25, 1998

1971

OPPOSITE: Astronaut Alan Shepard inspects the trophy, that was presented to him for his golfing exploits during the February 1971 *Apollo 14* mission to the Moon. Shepard received a "Golf All-America" award for his series of six-iron shots, which was viewed by millions during a live telecast from the lunar surface.

BELOW: *Apollo 14* astronaut Alan Shepard, center, prepares to swing at a golf ball on the lunar surface during a televised Moon Walk in February 1971. On the left is fellow astronaut and pilot Edgar Mitchell with the lunar module and the S-band antenna in the foreground.

His was the ultimate driving range, where it just did not matter which club he used. Astronaut Alan B. Shepard, Jr., commander of the *Apollo 14* Moon Mission, completed his mission by swinging his golf club in zero gravity, hitting two balls on the surface of the Moon. He was the first and remains the only person to accomplish this feat.

On May 5, 1961, Shepard flew a fifteen-minute suborbital flight over the Atlantic Ocean, becoming in the process the first American in space. In 1963, however, he developed an inner-ear disease, and was grounded. Shepard was put in charge of the Astronauts' office. Undeterred by his ailment, which was corrected by surgery, Shepard was determined to get back into space at least one more time. When, at age forty-seven, he was offered command of the *Apollo 14* mission, he eagerly accepted. The launch took place January 31, 1971.

The pressure suits worn by the Apollo astronauts while on the Moon hindered their mobility, especially their ability to bend over. For this reason, special tools were designed to allow them to collect rocks and soil for return to the Earth. One of these was the Contingency Sampling Tool, carried by the astronauts on their space suits, and designed specifically to allow them to pick up samples from an upright position. It is basically a collapsible handle with a collection bag at the end. It was this tool that became Alan Shepard's golf club. (He had had a little help from Jack Harden, at that time the head pro at River Oaks Country Club in Houston, who — sworn to secrecy — rigged the club for him.)

On the *Apollo 14* Mission, Shepard, along with astronaut Edward Mitchell, logged more than thirty-three hours trudging about on the Moon's surface in deep, shifting lunar dust. Neither slept a lick, and their final major task was to scale the flank of a crater while towing, pushing, and even carrying a cumbersome cart bearing tools and compartments for geological samples. It was heavy, joyless work. Pressured by the deadline and irritable from the lack of sleep, Shepard and Mitchell grew cranky. They muttered expletives from time to time, something that had seldom happened when the public was listening.

But when the work was finished, Shepard pulled out two golf balls and unfolded the collapsible golf club — to the considerable surprise of NASA officials. Despite thick gloves and a stiff suit that forced him to swing the club with one hand only, he shot a 200-yard (180m) drive on his second try. (The first shot went astray, rolling into a crater. Shepard commented simply, "Got more dirt than ball.")

Shepard recalled his pleasure in the moment. "I said, 'Miles and miles and miles!' which was a slight exaggeration. I folded up the club, with the clubhead, put it in my pocket, climbed up the ladder, closed the door and we took off."

On his return to earth, this casual golfer was featured on the cover of *Golf Magazine* as "Golf's Man on the Moon." His ersatz six-iron can still be viewed at the USGA Museum and Library in Far Hills, New Jersey.

The First Player to Win the Grand Slam Tournaments Twice

Jack Nicklaus

January 21, 1940 –

CAREER HIGHLIGHTS
U.S. Amateur: 1959, 1961;
U.S. Open: 1962, 1967,
1972, 1980; U.S. Masters:
1963, 1965-66, 1972, 1975,
1986; USPGA: 1963, 1971,
1973, 1975, 1980; British
Open: 1966, 1970, 1978;
Winner of 70 U.S. Tour
Events, 1962-86

World Golf Hall of Fame:
1974
Bob Jones Award: 1975
Player of The Century:
1988
Honorary Member of the
Royal & Ancient Golf Club

BELOW: Bernhard Langer
(left) applauds as Jack
Nicklaus, puts on his
record sixth Green Jacket.

OPPOSITE: Nicklaus,
at the British Open in 1975.

During his heyday and up to the present, Jack Nicklaus has held sway over golf in such a sweeping and innovative manner that he is considered one of the most influential figures in the history of the game. The aggregate impact Nicklaus has had on the game is astounding: Aside from racking up nearly 20 championships over his career, he has been a prolific course architect, as well as an ambassador to the game.

As a golfer Nicklaus has won every honor that there is — only the record for the highest number of USPGA tournament victories is missing from his trophy collection. His masterful touch as a course designer, particularly his ability to integrate stiff challenges for players of every skill level into the existing landscape, can be seen from Arizona to Japan.

In the 1971 PGA Championship at the PGA National in Palm Beach, at the ripe old age of thirty-one, Nicklaus won by two strokes over Billy Casper to capture his second USPGA title (he won a total of five, a record he shares with Walter Hagen). With that victory he also became the first player in the history of golf to win the Grand Slam tournaments two times.

Nicklaus took up golf at the age of ten. By the time he was nineteen he had won his first U.S. Amateur Championship — the youngest player in fifty years to do so — and was playing on the distinguished Walker Cup team. Two years later, in 1961, he won the Amateur again, after setting a record 282 for an amateur in the 1960 U.S. Open, finishing second to Arnold Palmer. He then turned pro. In 1962, he took the U.S. Open again.

The 1960s were golden years for the "Golden Bear," so-called because of his size and aggressive style of play. Nicklaus became the first golfer to win successive Masters, in 1965 and 1966. In his fifth Masters victory in 1975, relying on his steely resolve and superlative putting, he trumped Tom Weiskopf and Johnny Miller. On the last day of the tournament, the three met in a dogfight. The pivotal moment of the match came at the par-3 sixteenth hole, where Nicklaus holed a gigantic 40-foot (1.2m) putt for a birdie two. That stroke moved him into a tie for the lead with Tom Weiskopf, who was watching it all from the sixteenth tee. Weiskopf immediately followed that stroke by leaving his tee-shot short of the green, from which he took three more shots to get down. Nicklaus won the tournament by a stroke.

In 1986, though many thought his best playing days were over, Nicklaus won the Masters for the sixth time at the age of forty-six. That triumph at Augusta was the highlight of the twenty-fifth season of his remarkable professional career, and his final victory before joining the senior tour in 1990. He had played in one hundred major championships, finding his way to the top three a remarkable forty-five times. He had won eighteen

majors — seven more than any other player — and he had earned more money than anyone in the history of the game.

On the senior tour, Nicklaus has ten wins, including two at the U.S. Senior Open. His career as a brilliant player has undoubtedly enhanced his work as a course designer. His courses regularly make "Best of" lists, and *Golf World* has named him "Architect of the Year." He co-designed a course with Arnold Palmer in St. Augustine, Florida, that is known as The King and Bear. Nicklaus also found time to pen an autobiography, *My Story*, in 1997.

It is impossible to overestimate Nicklaus' impact on the game. Perhaps Frank Deford said it best: "How many other champions have become so identified with their sport, with the very essence of it, that it is impossible to think of one without the other?"

The First African-American to Play the Masters
Lee Elder

July 14, 1934–

CAREER HIGHLIGHTS
PGA Tour: 4 victories
1974-1978; Senior PGA
Tour: 8 victories 1984-1988;
Ryder Cup: 1979

BELOW: Lee Elder, the
first African-American golfer
to qualify for the Masters,
leaves the historic clubhouse
before practicing for the
tournament in 1975.

OPPOSITE: Lee Elder
is ecstatic after holing
an 18-foot (5.5m) birdie
putt on the fourth hole
of a sudden-death playoff
to beat Englishman Peter
Ooserhuis and win the
Monsanto Open in
Pensacola, Florida, in 1974.

More than a quarter century ago, Lee Elder penetrated the pearly-white bastion of Augusta National, becoming the first African-American to play in the Masters Tournament. In so doing, he opened the doors for many talented athletes who followed him, most notably Tiger Woods, whose victories in 1997 and 2000 were graced by Elder's presence.

Born Robert Lee Elder in Dallas, Texas, Lee didn't have an easy time growing up. He lost both parents at an early age — his father was killed in combat in World War II, and his mother died soon afterwards. Elder and his seven siblings were uprooted, and finally resettled with a relative in Los Angeles. As a youngster, already having developed an affinity for golf, Elder started to work as a caddy at clubs around San Bernardino, California.

Elder dropped out of school altogether and began not only to caddy full time, but also to hustle a golf game or two. Moses Brooks, another African-American golf hustler, took Elder under his wing. They went back to Dallas, where Elder earned attention by winning under such bizarre handicaps as playing on his knees or on one leg. He later paired up with famed hustler Titanic Thompson, posing as Thompson's caddy. Thompson would bet his foes that even his caddy could beat them, after which the stakes were increased. Elder would step up to the tee, and the "caddy" would cruise to victory over his shocked opponents.

Elder's golfing skills received another lift in 1959 from a highly unlikely source: the U.S. Army. After being drafted, Elder was fortunate enough to wind up at Fort Lewis, Washington. Commanding officer Colonel John Gleaster, an avid golfer, proceeded to put Elder on "golf duty," assigning him to a special services unit where Elder could play golf on a steady basis for sixteen months. While in the service, Elder won the championship of his post twice, placed second in the All-Service Tournament in 1960, and lost to future U.S. Open champion Orville Moody in the Sixth Army Championship.

By the time he was discharged from the army in 1961, Elder had honed his game sufficiently that he felt ready to turn professional. He joined the United Golf Association (UGA) Tour of professional black players, and won the championship five times. During one stretch he had a remarkable run of twenty-one victories in twenty-three consecutive tournaments. Unfortunately, little income could be earned on this circuit, which was known as the "Peanut Tour" due to winners' shares being as low as $500. Many of the tournaments were held on public courses that received nowhere near the maintenance of private country clubs.

After raising the necessary funds ($6,500) by working as a golf instructor, in 1967 Elder became the second African-American (Charlie Sifford was the first) to qualify and play for the Professional Golfers' Association (PGA) Tour. His record in the PGA includes four victories.

Until 1974, the Masters was an invitational tournament, and although considerable public pressure had been put on Augusta National Chairman, Clifford Roberts, to include Elder, no invitation had been issued. When the rules changed so that any PGA event winner automatically qualified, however, the lack of an invitation ceased to matter. Elder won the 1974 Monsanto Open, and the next year he became the first African-American to play at Augusta. Though he did not take home a victory, he went on to play in five more Masters tournaments.

Elder was also the first African-American to be invited to play in the South African PGA Open (1971), and the first African-American to qualify for the prestigious Ryder Cup Golf team (1979). In 1984 Elder joined the PGA Senior Tour, where he has won eight titles and earned more than one million dollars. His last victory came at the 1988 Gus Machado Classic.

The First Player to Break 70 for All Four Rounds in a U.S. Open

Lee Trevino

December 1, 1939 –

1968

CAREER HIGHLIGHTS
U.S. Open: 1968, 1971;
British Open: 1971-72;
Canadian Open: 1971,
1977, 1979; USPGA: 1974,
1984; U.S. Players
Championship: 1980;
British Masters: 1985;
U.S. Senior Open: 1990;
USPGA Seniors': 1992,
1994; World Cup: 1968-71,
1974 (Individual Winner
1969); Ryder Cup: 1969-75,
1979-81 (Non-playing
Captain 1985)

Vardon Trophy: 1970-72,
1974, 1980.
World Golf Hall of
Fame: 1981

RIGHT: Jack Nicklaus (left)
and Lee Trevino walk off
the 18th green at Merion
Golf Club in Ardmore,
Pennsylvania, in 1971, after
Trevino defeated Nicklaus
in an extra 18-hole round
for the U.S. Open title.

OPPOSITE: Lee Trevino
reacts favorably after he
birdied the fourth hole in
the third round of the U.S.
Open Golf Championship
at the Merion Golf Club
at Ardmore, Pennsylvania,
in 1971.

f it weren't for the location of his family home — a four-room plank house that stood in a hayfield next to the Glen Lakes Country Club in Dallas, Texas — Lee Trevino probably would have never picked up the game.

Raised by his mother, a housecleaner, and his grandfather, a gravedigger, Trevino grew up in an impoverished family. His first golf earnings came from finding stray balls. In 1994, his highest-earning year, he won $1,202,369. As he made his journey to affluence, he never forgot how and where he was raised.

"Rich people like to talk about their backgrounds," Trevino said. "We were just too poor to care. We just managed to exist."

Trevino's attraction to the golf course led him to begin caddying at the age of eight. Hanging around the caddy shack, he basically taught himself to golf. At seventeen, he joined the U.S. Marine Corps, where he was lucky enough to be able to continue honing his golfing skills. In one of his rounds there, he shot a nifty 66. When his unit transferred abroad to Asia, he played in Japan, Taiwan, and the Philippines.

Upon returning home to Texas after his discharge in 1961, Trevino, like Lee Elder, started to hustle in local matches. He would rope opponents in by using one club—a beat-up but reliable three-iron — over an entire round. But when playtime was over, Trevino turned professional, and gave a new set of opponents their share of licks.

It was a long time before Trevino made any impact on the U.S. Tour. In 1967, he earned a respectable fifth place in the U.S. Open and was named Rookie of the Year, which persuaded him to join the Tour full time.

He was basically an unknown when he came to the 1968 Open at Oak Hill, Rochester, .and won in spectacular fashion, defeating the illustrious Jack Nicklaus by four strokes and becoming the first player to break 70 in all four rounds of the championship. After that inspiring showing, the golfing world welcomed this unconventional character, with his idiosyncratic style of play, as a major new superstar — in fact, they called him "Supermex."

Along with his newfound fame, Trevino quickly developed a reputation as a jokester. While waiting to tee off in a playoff for the 1971 U.S. Open, he reached into the golf bag and pulled out a rubber snake, which he lobbed at Nicklaus. The Golden Bear momentarily looked worried, until he realized the reptile wasn't real. Whether he was spooked by the snake, we don't know, but Nicklaus made a disappointing start to this head-to-head duel, dropping three strokes in the first three holes. Four hours later Trevino had won his second U.S. Open title by three shots, 68 to 71.

Trevino reached his peak in the early 1970s. He had a group of dedicated fans — "Lee's fleas" — who followed his every move. At the start of the decade, he was the leading money winner on the U.S. Tour; in 1971 he won three Opens — the United States, British, and Canadian — in a four-week span. He was the first to accomplish that feat.

His luck took a dive in 1975, when Trevino was hit by lightning while playing in the Western Open in Chicago. Though his back was injured, and he underwent several surgeries, Trevino fought to rebuild his game. In 1977, he came back to win the Canadian Open, and repeated that feat in 1979. In 1984, at the age of forty-four, Trevino took the PGA title.

In 1989, Trevino switched to the Senior tour. In 1990, he won more money on the Senior Tour than the winner of the regular U.S. Tour.

Still, despite all his extraordinary victories and substantial earnings, Trevino never forgot his origins: "A lot of guys on the Tour gripe about the travel and the food, and losing their laundry, but no matter how bad the food is, I've eaten worse. And I couldn't care less about the dry cleaning because I remember when I only had one shirt."

The First LPGA Professional To Earn More Than $100,000 in a Single Season

Judy Rankin

February 18, 1945 –

1976

CAREER HIGHLIGHTS

Vare Trophy: 1973,
1976, 1977
Patty Berg Award: 1999
LPGA Hall of Fame: 2000
World Golf Hall of
Fame: 2000
Bob Jones Award: 2002

OPPOSITE: Judy Rankin,
leading money winner on
the Ladies Tour in 1976,
tees off on the fifth hole
of the first round of the
Women's U.S. Open in
Springfield, Pennsylvania.

BELOW: Judy Rankin,
a LPGA Hall of Fame
member, is now a golf
analyst and commentator
for ABC Sports.

The frequent trips six-year-old Judy took to the golfing range with her father certainly paid off.

Out-finessing men and women alike on a closest-to-the-pin contest, crushing the preteens in a National Pee Wee Golf championship, and having a golfing trophy renamed in her honor are just a few of the early triumphs of Judy Rankin's life — all earned before the St. Louis, Missouri, native turned ten years old.

Rankin's teenage successes confirmed her wondrous ability. In 1959, she again stunned her peers by winning the Missouri State Amateur. She still holds the record as that event's youngest champion. At the age of sixteen, Rankin even graced the cover of *Sports Illustrated*.

These impressive outings were a precursor to what Rankin would do later as a professional. She joined the LPGA in 1962, and rose steadily to become one of the top golfers of her day.

Her first win came in 1968, and was followed by twenty-five more over the next fourteen years. In 1973, she captured four tournaments and finished second on the money list. It was clear that she had found her stroke, as she won the first of three Vare Trophies (the others came in 1976 and '77) for the lowest stroke average over an entire season.

In 1976 Rankin became the first woman to win $100,000 or more in a single season. That year she got off to a rapid start as she won her first event of the season in Miami, Florida. Then, in April, she redeemed herself at the Dinah Shore Classic, the same tournament in which a few years earlier she had blown a lead earned on the front nine when she falterd on the backend. In this Classic, battling the brutal cold and blustery winds, she came from three strokes off the pace the final day to shoot a 68. During the telecast, ABC Sports announcer Bob Rosberg emphasized her achievement: "Considering these conditions, this may be one of the greatest rounds ever played." Rankin won four more times that year and earned a record $150,724, shattering the previous mark by more than $60,000.

The end of the 1977 season would mark the end of Rankin's five-year reign as the best woman golfer in the world; her record of twenty-five top-ten finishes in a season still stands. From 1973 to 1977, she won more tournaments (seventeen), had higher earnings ($442,669), and earned the lowest stroke average (72.89) on the LPGA Tour.

Near the end of the decade, Rankin's play began to decline as burnout and back pain took their toll on the superstar. In 1983 Rankin retired from the tour, and though she no longer plays professionally, she is still is very much involved in the game. Since 1984, she has become well known as a golf announcer and analyst for ABC Sports. She captained two winning Solheim Cup teams, in 1986 and 1988. As an ambassador of the game, she has been tireless: her contributions were recognized when she won the Bob Jones Award in 2002.

The First Woman to Win the Modern-Day Grand Slam

Pat Bradley

March 21, 1951 –

1986

CAREER HIGHLIGHTS

Peter Jackson Classic: 1980;
U.S. Women's Open: 1981;
Du Maurier Classic: 1985,
1986; Nabisco Dinah Shore:
1986; LPGA Championship:
1986

Rolex Player of the Year:
1986, 1991
Vare Trophy: 1986, 1991
William and Mousie
Powell Award: 1991
World Golf Hall of
Fame: 1991
LPGA Hall of Fame: 1992

OPPOSITE: Pat Bradley
rejoices after sinking a
difficult birdie putt on
the 18th hole to take the
lead in the third round
of the Nabisco Dinah
Shore LPGA tournament at
Rancho Mirage, California,
in April 1986.

Throughout her illustrious career, Pat Bradley has been the standard-bearer of her sport, even in the face of a devastating disease, which almost ended her reign on the links — and her life.

Bradley's feats are undoubtedly more impressive considering that at the peak of her career in 1988, she was stricken with Graves Disease, a debilitating thyroid condition, which went undetected for a year and caused a precipitous drop in her ranking from first place in money ranking to number 109. After receiving medical treatment, Bradley found her way back to the top spot.

Soon after battling back from her ailment and before reclaiming the number one ranking, she hosted her own tournament, the Planters Pat Bradley International in High Point, North Carolina. Two years later in 1990, she surpassed the $3 million career earning mark, and proceeded to go over the $4 million plateau in 1991. Bradley was the first LPGA player to reach those earning marks.

In Bradley's twenty-five plus years on the Tour, she has racked up more than thirty tournament victories, including six majors. Moreover, she is a two-time LPGA Player of the Year (1986, '91), and has won all four majors on the LPGA Tour, including three du Maurier Classics. Bradley is among all-time LPGA money leaders and tournament winners — in all she's won thirty-one tournaments.

Bradley's achievements have gained her a place in the LPGA Hall of Fame, one of the most exclusive clubs in professional sports. She was officially inducted as the 12th member of the LPGA Tour Hall of Fame on January 18, 1992, in Boston. Upon her induction into the Hall, the Bradley family donated a Swiss cowbell that her mother would ring on the back porch of the family home in Westford, Massachusetts, whenever Pat won. The bell rang out for every victory, from the very first at the Colegate Far East Open in 1975, until the thirtieth at the MBS LPGA Classic in 1991, which qualified Bradley for induction into the Hall. That bell can be seen at the World Golf Hall of Fame in St. Augustine, Florida, home of the LPGA Tour Hall of Fame.

It was at Los Coyotes Country Club in Buena Park, California, that Bradley won the MBS LPGA Classic in 1991 to qualify for the Hall of Fame. It had been a dream of her father's to see his daughter inducted. But sadly, Richard Bradley never saw his daughter make it to the Hall. He died in 1988, the same year that Pat was stricken with Graves Disease. After rebounding from the emotional loss of her father and her own debilitating health problems, she won one tournament in 1989, three in 1990, and another three in 1991, giving her twenty-nine career victories, one shy of the thirty needed for qualification. At the MBS LPGA Classic she started the final round four strokes back. With victory in doubt and immortality in the balance, Bradley stormed back and took the lead on Sunday with a birdie at the 13th hole and won the tournament by one stroke. She had finally fulfilled her father's dream, and her own. She was a member of the Hall of Fame.

But perhaps Bradley's finest achievement had come when she completed the modern-day grand slam with a victory at the LPGA Championship in 1986. She took the championship, edging out Patty Sheehan, another Hall of Famer, with an 11-under 277 at the Jack Nicklaus Sports Center in Kings Island,

Ohio. 1986 was a great year for Bradley; in addition to the LPGA Championship, she also won the Nabisco Dinah Shore Championship, and her third du Maurier Classic to become the only LPGA player in history to win three of the four modern-day majors in a single season.

Bradley was a member of the 1990, 1992, and 1996 U.S. Solheim Cup teams and she served as captain for the team in 2000. She was also a recipient of the 1991 Golf Writers Association of America's Ben Hogan Award for her comeback after suffering from Graves Disease. The award is given annually to an individual who has continued to be active in golf despite a physical handicap or serious illness. A great long iron player, Bradley holds the LPGA record for the lowest 54-hole score, 197, and shares the record for the lowest 9-hole score, 28.

Before turning to golf, Bradley mined her talents as a competitive skier and ski instructor. Later she attended Florida International University, where she was an All-American golfer in 1970.

Bradley's amateur career was spent in her native New England area. She won the New Hampshire Amateur in 1967 and 1969 and the New England Amateur in 1972-73. But her professional career got off to a relatively slow start. After joining the LPGA Tour in 1974, Bradley went without a win in her rookie season. She won her first unofficial event the next year, but she would have to wait until 1976 for her first sponsored event title at the Girl Talk Classic, where she defeated Judy Rankin, Bonnie Lauer, and Sandra Post on the second hole of a sudden-death playoff. From there her career took off. In 1978, Bradley recorded the first of eight multiple-win seasons.

Her success can be attributed to a solid all-around game and a concentration so intense that the "Bradley Stare" is legendary on the LPGA tour. Consistency is another Bradley trademark, for she has finished in the top ten of more than half of the five hundred-plus tournaments she has entered, and she has more than fifty second-place finishes. Among her many awards are two Vare Trophies for lowest season scoring average, and two Player of the Year Awards, as well as being recognized as one of the LPGA's top fifty players and teachers at the LPGA's Fiftieth Anniversary in 2000.

2002 marks Bradley's start on the Women's Senior Golf Tour. There is little doubt that she'll leave her indelible stamp on that tour, just as she has on the world of women's golf.

OPPOSITE: Pat Bradley tees off on November 6, 1981, on the final hole of the 5,765-meter, at the Sagamihara Country Club, west of Tokyo.

BELOW: Pat Bradley, holds her LPGA Player of the Year Award on November 18, 1986, at New York's Pierre Hotel. Bradley won the LPGA Series Award and the Vare Trophy to become only the second player to make a clean sweep of the major annual LPGA awards.

The First-Ever World Number One Golfer

Bernhard Langer

August 27, 1957 –

1986

CAREER HIGHLIGHTS
European Tour wins: 34
Ryder Cup: 1981–95
World Golf Hall of Fame:
2002

BELOW: Langer raises his arms in his newly outfitted green jacket after winning the 1993 U.S. Masters Championship at Augusta National.

OPPOSITE: Germany's Bernhard Langer, known for his putting yips, places the ball on the green for a putt during round two of the 1994 British

When the inaugural Sony Ranking was published in April 1986, Bernhard Langer of Anhausen, Germany, had the honor of being the first-ever world number one player. While Sony was the sponsor of the ranking system, it was International Management Group (IMG) founder and chairman Mark McCormack, whose handshake in 1960 with golf giant Arnold Palmer enabled the creation of this massive agency. It began devising the formula to determine who would be the world's number one golfer as early as 1968.

The formula ranking, which is sanctioned by the Championship Committee of the Royal & Ancient Golf Club of St. Andrews, is computed on a two-year rolling points basis weighted toward the current year. Players earn points based on tournament grade, finish, and strength of field. The four majors are worth fifty points for the winner, thirty for second place, and twenty for third, continuing down to one point for forty-third place and everyone who makes the cut.

Points for other tournaments are decided by how many of the top one hundred players are in the field. So a tournament such as the Bay Hill Invitational, traditionally one of the stronger fields on the strongest tour in golf, will be worth substantially more than the Portuguese Open. And if a field is particularly weak, points may be awarded only to the top ten finishers.

Bonus points are awarded to a tournament that has the top thirty money-winners on its respective tour in the field. Also, each tour has its own flagship event worth a minimum number of points: The Players Championship (forty points), the Volvo Masters (thirty-two points), the Australian and Japanese Opens (sixteen points each).

Since 1997, golf's major professional organizations have endorsed the Official World Golf Rankings. In 1999, the governing body of the World Golf Rankings installed the McCormack Award to recognize each year that player who was in the Number One position for the most number of weeks during the year.

Langer, who held onto his first-place ranking for the first three weeks of the 1986 season, is the player who put Germany on the world golf map. The son of a bricklayer, Langer began his golf career as a caddy. He was eight years old, and hoping to supplement the family income with his earnings. By fourteen, he was offered a position as assistant pro at the Munich Golf Club. In 1974, he won the German National Open, and in 1976 joined the PGA's European Tour. By 1981, he was consistently winning tournaments all over Europe.

The auspicious prelude to his crowning as World Number One came in 1985. He tore up the links that year, winning several tournaments, including the Masters. What sealed his top status in that tournament was a key moment at the par-4 seventeenth in the final round, when Langer holed a birdie putt from 14 feet (4.2m). It allowed him the luxury of taking a bogey five at the final hole and still winning the title. Langer won the Masters again eight years later, that time by four shots. The decisive moment was an eagle three at the thirteenth, when Langer sank a tricky downhill putt.

At the top of his game, Langer was afflicted with a problem known as "the yips," in which the player cannot control his hands on the putter. It took great effort to overcome, and Langer continues to experiment with different putters. He has no fewer than forty European Tour titles, and in 2002 became the first German player to be elected to the World Golf Hall of Fame.

The First Golfer to Lose His Knickers in a Bet

Payne Stewart

January 30, 1957 – October 25, 1999

1988

CAREER HIGHLIGHTS
USPGA: 1989;
U.S. Open: 1991, 1999;
Dutch Open: 1991

Four Tours Championship: 1986-87, 1989-90; Ryder Cup: 1987-93, 1999
World Cup: 1987, 1990; Dunhill Cup: 1993, 1999

BELOW: The late Payne Stewart exults after nailing a putt at the 1999 U.S. Open at Pinehurst No. 2 in Pinehurst, North Carolina. He went on to win the tournament, his first U.S. Open title.

OPPOSITE: Payne Stewart works out of the bunker during the 1999 British Open played at the Carnoustie Golf Club in Carnoustie, Scotland.

His unmistakable flair was displayed from his vibrantly colored tam-o'-shanter caps down through the brightly colored jerseys to the gold-tipped shoes on his feet. He was one of the few players of the modern era to wear plus-fours, or knickers, on the course. The flashy dress was truly an extension of Payne Stewart's personality: colorful, exuberant, and animated.

The Springfield, Missouri, native was an immense crowd favorite, loved for both his talent and his antics.

Before playing an exhibition match in 1988 at the Hercules Country Club in Wilmington, Delaware, he made a typically outrageous wager.

He bet three women professionals that he could beat their best ball. If he lost he would remove his knickers; if they lost, they would have to take off their shorts. On the final hole he lost the bet and, to the delight of the spectators, removed his knickers.

Stewart began golfing at the age of four, taught by his father, who had been an amateur state champion. He grew up to join the PGA Tour in 1982, and was a top-notch player for two decades. By 1989, he topped the $1 million earnings mark, was an established U.S. Ryder Cup player, and had won his first major title, the USPGA. Two years later he defeated Scott Simpson for his second major. Both had finished six under par after seventy-two holes before Stewart went on to win the title by two strokes in the 18-hole playoff.

In 1998, Stewart lost a U.S. Open title to Lee Janzen that he should have won; however, the following year he redeemed himself by capturing the title at the Pinehurst's famous Number 2 course. Stewart dropped a breathtaking, snakey putt on the final green to fend off Phil Mickelson by one stroke to secure the 1999 U.S. Open title. It was the longest putt ever to win the Open on the deciding hole.

Stewart died tragically in a plane crash at the age of forty-two, only weeks after winning his second U.S. Open title in 1999. He had boarded a chartered, twin-engine Lear 35, and was on his way to Texas to discuss a proposed new course near Dallas. From there, he was to play in the Tour Championship in Houston for the top thirty on the USPGA Tour's money list. The aircraft suffered a loss of cabin pressure, and flew a ghastly journey halfway across the United States with its windows iced over until it came down in a field in South Dakota. All six of the people aboard were lost.

"My father always said the easiest way to set yourself apart in a crowd is by the way you dress," noted Stewart, but he is remembered for much more than his sartorial skill.

The First Player to Win More than $1,000,000 in a Single Season
Curtis Strange

January 30, 1955–

CAREER HIGHLIGHTS

Canadian Open 1985, 1987;
U.S. Open 1988, 1989; U.S.
Tour Championship 1988
PGA Tour: 17 victories
1979-89

Eisenhower Trophy: 1974
Walker Cup: 1975
Ryder Cup: 1983-89, 1995
(Captain 2001)
Four Tours Championship:
1985, 1987-89, Dunhill Cup
1987-91, 1994
Arnold Palmer Award:
1985, 1987, 1988
USGA Player of the Year:
1988

BELOW: Curtis Strange
tees off on the fifth
hole during a practice
round for the 76th PGA
Championship at Southern
Hills Golf Club in Tulsa,
Oklahoma, in 1994.

OPPOSITE: Curtis Strange
kisses his trophy, which
he won by taking the 1998
U.S. Open.

The benchmark had its merits, but capturing his first major was what really made 1988 a year that Curtis Strange would treasure.

After Strange notched a win at the season-ending Nabisco Championships at Pebble Beach in 1988, and collected the $360,000 paycheck there, it lifted his official Tour earnings to $1,147,644, thereby making him the first million-plus dollar player in a single season.

As the son of a professional golfer in Norfolk, Virginia, Strange came to the game at an early age, playing almost daily from the age of eight. As an amateur, he was known for his booming drives. When he was nineteen, Strange was selected for the Eisenhower Trophy team, and the following year he played in the U.S. Walker Cup victory over Great Britain and Ireland.

Strange turned professional in 1976 at the age of twenty-one and qualified for the U.S. Tour a year later. But that year, as well as the next, Strange toiled at the bottom of the money list and had difficulty righting his swing. He knew that in order to make his stroke more reliable, he had to sacrifice some distance.

The time spent correcting his swing paid off: by the end of the decade, Strange was becoming a force. He won his first U.S. Tour event in 1979, and the next year finished third in the U.S. money list. He was runner-up in the Masters in 1985 and runner-up in the USPGA Championship in Kemper Lakes in 1989.

Strange's consecutive U.S. Open wins in 1988 and 1989 catapulted the golfer to the rarefied heights. He was the first golfer since Ben Hogan in 1950 and 1951 to take back-to-back U.S. Opens.

After a string of near misses in major championships, Curtis Strange buckled down in the 1988 U.S. Open at The

Country Club in Brookline, Massachusetts, where he beat England's Nick Faldo in an 18-hole playoff. The crucial moment in the tournament came at the thirteenth, where Strange sank an 18-foot (5.5m) birdie putt, while Faldo bogied to fall three back of Strange. Although Faldo birdied the fourteenth, he then proceeded to drop three shots to par over the final four holes. Strange won 71-75.

In 1989's U.S. Open at Oak Hill in Rochester, New York, Strange was at it again, beating Tom Kite, who was the leader going into the final round. A poor round left him five strokes behind Strange.

Since 1992, Strange has been an on-air analyst for ABC Sports golfing events. He also holds the record of 62 — 10 under par — for the Old Course at St. Andrews.

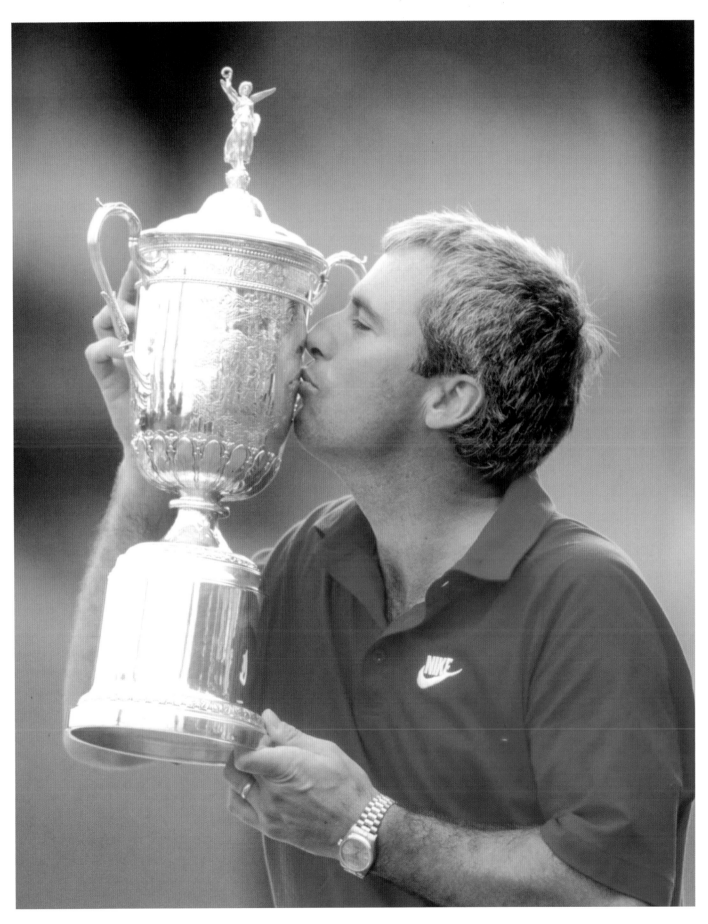

The First Player to be Granted Use of a Golf Cart During Play

Casey Martin

June 2, 1972–

1998

Ever since the controversial decision was handed down in 1998, many in the golfing world, as well as the larger community, have been split on whether using a cart during play violates the basic tenets of the sport.

Casey Martin has a rare disorder that affects the circulation in his right leg — an affliction that makes it painful and even dangerous to walk — but he also has immense talent as a golfer. Before the age of fourteen, he won seventeen Oregon Golf Association junior events, and went on to play on the Stanford University team with Tiger Woods. He turned pro in 1995.

When his condition had deteriorated to the point that he could not walk the course without severe pain, Martin asked the PGA for permission to use a golf cart during competition. When the PGA refused his request, Martin took golf's ruling body to court. In February 1998, a U.S. Magistrate found in Martin's favor, and that ruling was upheld by the 9th U.S. Circuit Court of Appeals in March 2001. The PGA appealed the ruling to the Supreme Court, and on May 29, 2001, the court ruled by a 7-2 vote that Casey has a legal right to ride a cart in PGA tour events. The judges ruled that Casey was protected under the 1990 Americans with Disabilities Act, which prohibits discrimination against disabled persons in public accommodations.

It was a landmark victory in the first case invoking federal disabilities laws in a major sport. The original ruling by Thomas Coffin found that a golf course during a tournament is a place of public accommodation. Coffin stated that Martin's lawyers had proved the golfer is disabled and entitled to a reasonable accommodation, which could include a cart.

"I just want to be given the chance to play, and I'm grateful for that chance now," said Martin in a news conference after the decision. "I was riding an emotional roller coaster for awhile, but I'm grateful it turned out like it did."

"I understand why (the PGA Tour) had to pursue this like they did," Martin added. "I never really had any animosity toward the Tour like they were treating me that poorly. If they were I forgive them."

The issue for the PGA Tour, and those who have sided with the association, was the possibility that giving Martin a cart would give him an unfair advantage. They were also concerned that the introduction of carts would lessen the fundamental need for athleticism and stamina that walking brings to top-flight tournament golf. But Coffin, who deliberated just a couple of hours, ruled that giving Martin a cart would not significantly alter the sport.

As for Martin himself, because of the severity of his condition, even walking to and from the cart requires great effort, and he has to wear a support to keep down the swelling in his leg. Nevertheless, he was a member of the PGA Tour in 2000 and the Buy.com Tour in 1998-99 and 2001; in the latter, he made the cut in nine of twenty-one tournaments entered.

The First LPGA Player to Break 60

Annika Sorenstam

October 9, 1970 –

2001

CAREER HIGHLIGHTS
World Amateur: 1992; U.S.
Women's Open: 1995,
1996; Nabisco
Championship: 2001, 2002

Rolex Rookie of the Year:
1994
Rolex Player of the Year:
1995, 1997, 1998, 2001
Vare Trophy: 1995, 1996,
1998, 2001

OPPOSITE: Annika
Sorenstam receives her
trophy for her win at
the Aerus Electrolux USA
Championship where
she beat Pat Hurst by
one stroke.

BELOW: Annika
Sorenstam follows
her shot on the 18th
hole during the third
round at the
Canadian Women's
Open LPGA at the
Angus Glen Golf Club
in Markham, Ontario,
on August 18, 2001.

magine, you are newly arrived in the Professional ranks, up from the Amateurs and the first win you seal is the LPGA's most prized tournament: The U.S. Open. That was Annika Sorenstam's seamless transition into professional golf in 1995 — and her game has only gotten better. A year later in 1996, she duplicated the act and put her stamp on the Tour as a legitimate player.

The Swedish phenom joined the LPGA in 1994 and has been a benchmark for superior play since her arrival. At thirty-one, Sorenstam was already the all-time LPGA money winner and had won more tournaments (eighteen) than any other player in the 90s. In 2001, Sorenstam set or tied thirty LPGA records, in part because of her unprecedented second-round 59 at that year's Standard Register PING.

Sorenstam shot her record 59 at the 2001 Standard Register PING held at Moon Valley Country Club in Phoenix, Arizona. It was the second round of the tournament and Sorenstam came out swinging; she started out shooting birdies on the first four holes, finishing with 5 on the front nine. After the turn, Sorenstam completed her record-setting run by shooting eight birdies in a row before finishing with a solid two-putt par on the par four 18th. She finished the round with thirteen birdies, setting a record for birdies in a round by two. This record also ties the PGA record of 59, held by Al Geiberger, Chip Beck, and David Duval. All told, Sorenstam's round broke four records and tied three. Records broken include: 18-hole raw score (59); 18-hole score in relation to par (13-under 59); 36-hole score (20-under 124); and most birdies in a round (13). Tied records include: most consecutive birdies (eight); nine-hole score in relation to par (8-under); and raw nine-hole score (28).

After her strong college career, Sorenstam competed on the WPG European tour, where she received the 1993 Rookie of the Year honors. In 1994 she was named the LPGA Rookie of the Year, only the second foreign player to receive the award. Sorenstam and Nancy Lopez are the only players to have received the Player of the Year honors followed the next year by the Rookie of the Year award.

In 1998 Sorenstam again won the Player of the Year award, her third in four seasons. That year also brought her third Vare Trophy for lowest scoring average, a 69.99 in twenty-one events, making her the first woman player to break 70.

Sorenstam started playing golf at the age of twelve, and credits her parents and her sister, Charlotta, also an LPGA Tour member, as the individuals who most influenced her career. She is only one of two players (Karrie Webb is the other) to win $1 million in earnings for three consecutive years. She is also the first foreign player to win the Vare Trophy for the lowest scoring average.

One of Sorenstam's contemporaries and chief rivals since bursting onto the Tour has been Webb, who outpaced the Swede in 1999, winning seven tournaments, captured her first Player of the Year Award, and became recognized as the world's most acknowledged female player.

Webb's play certainly motivated Sorenstam to elevate her game, even as it appeared she had already reached the pinnacle of success. Sorenstam realized she'd have to further hone her body while simultaneously pushing farther off the tee in order to compete with Webb and the rest of the field constantly at her heels.

A member of the Swedish National Team from 1987-92, Sorenstam enjoyed a very successful amateur career. In 1992, she was the World Amateur champion, runner-up at the U.S. Women's Amateur and the second-lowest amateur at the U.S. Women's Open. In addition to winning seven collegiate titles during her career at the University of Arizona, she was the 1991 NCAA Co-College Player of the Year (with Kelly Robbins), 1991 NCAA champion and runner-up the following year, 1992 PAC-10 champion and 1991-92 NCAA All-American.

While Sorenstam has not won the Grand Slam yet, it seems inevitable that one day she'll conquer that as well.

OPPOSITE: Annika Sorenstam's putt falls for a birdie on the 18th hole at the Aerus Electrolux USA Championship on May 9, 2002, in Franklin, Tennessee.

BELOW: Annika Sorenstam stands proud at the LPGA Standard Register PING Tournament on March 16, 2001, in Phoenix, Arizona, where she shot her record-breaking 59. The scoreboard behind her shows her record round.

The First to Hold All Four Majors at Once

Tiger Woods

December 30, 1975–

CAREER HIGHLIGHTS

U.S. Amateur 1994-96;
U.S. Masters 1997, 2001;
2002; USPGA 1999, 2000;
WGC Invitational 1999,
2000; U.S. Tour
Championship 1999;
WGC Stroke-play 1999;
U.S. Open 2000; 2002
British Open 2000;
WGC Team 2000, 2001;
U.S. Players; PGA Tour:
24 victories 1996-2000

Arnold Palmer Award
1997, 1999, 2000
USPGA Player Of The Year
1997, 1999, 2000
Vardon Trophy 1999, 2000
Ryder Cup 1997-99

RIGHT: Tiger Woods
and caddy Steve Williams
celebrate on the green
after Tiger wins the 2001
Masters.

OPPOSITE: Tiger gets
help with his second green
jacket from Vijay Singh after
winning the 2001 Masters.

The truism "Youth is wasted on the young" doesn't apply to Tiger Woods, whose youthful achievements surpass those belonging to many long and illustrious careers. His collection of "firsts" outranks any other.

After turning pro in 1996, it wouldn't be long before Tiger would ascend to the top of the golf ranks. Before scalding the competition in the amateur ranks in 1995, Tiger played in his first PGA Tournament that same year, and was the only amateur to make the cut in that match. He finished in forty-first place.

Immediately after he became a professional, at just twenty years old, and with zero majors to his credit, Tiger nevertheless contracted a $40 million deal with Nike and a $20 million deal with Titleist.

Although he reached the age of twenty-one in 1997, becoming "legal," his play was so astonishing that it sometimes seemed to both his fans and peers as if it should be outlawed. That year, he captured his first Masters and set a record for earnings with $2,066,833.

Those earnings came largely from his Masters victory. Four years later, in 2001, Tiger was outfitted for another green jacket as he captured a second Masters Tournament. Sandwiched in between those victories, the prodigy notched wins at the 1999 and 2000 PGA Championships, the 2000 U.S. Open Championship, and the 2000 British Open Championship. With his second Masters victory in 2001, in a fierce duel against David Duval and Phil Mickelson on the tournament's final day, Tiger became the first player ever to hold all four professional major championships at the same time. In 2002, he took the Masters once more, joining the ranks of the few but proud defending Masters champions.

Woods, whose given name is Eldrick, was nicknamed "Tiger" for a Vietnamese soldier friend of his father, Earl Woods, a retired lieutenant colonel in the U.S. Army. Tiger was already on a prodigious path as a toddler, exchanging his baby shoes for golf spikes.

He was putting against Bob Hope at the age of two on *The Mike Douglas Show*. A year later, he had shot 48 for nine holes; by five years old, he was a feature subject in the magazine *Golf Digest*.

Encouraged by his father, Tiger conquered the teenage ranks to become one of junior golf's most accomplished players. He won several major youth titles in his native California before capturing three straight Junior Amateur Titles beginning in 1991 (the youngest winner ever of that title). Tiger capped his amateur play by making history in 1996 with three consecutive Amateur Championships (once again, the youngest ever to win that title).

His four-round total of 270 at the Masters shattered almost every

record for low scoring, including the lowest winning score, the widest winning margin (he won by nine strokes), and the youngest winner of the famous green jacket at twenty-one years, three months, and fifteen days — a record previously held by Seve Ballesteros, whose win came at the age of twenty-three years and three days in 1980.

Tiger shattered the record books with his win at the 2000 U.S. Open. He set the mark for margin of victory at fifteen shots, became the first player to finish in double digits under par at 12-under, and matched the all-time score of 272. With his

second U.S. open win in 2002 he garnered his eighth USGA championship, tying him with Jack Nicklaus and bringing him in one behind Bobby Jones.

In addition to a tireless work ethic, Tiger's success derives from the way he maximizes his physical abilities: when he puts it all together, his game is an awesome spectacle to behold.

Since he has stormed the professional ranks, his impact has been infectious — even non-golfers have taken a shine to the sport because of the "Tiger Factor." And when Tiger's on the tube, Nielsen Ratings and advertising revenue always seem to climb.

The First Woman To Earn $1 Million for a Season

Karrie Webb

December 21, 1974 –

1996

OPPOSITE: Karrie Webb blasts from the sand trap on the second green during the first round in the LPGA Tour Championship at the Desert Inn Golf Course in Las Vegas on November 21, 1996.

Since bursting onto the LPGA scene in 1996, Karrie Webb has made her case as one of the most talented women golfers ever to player the game. Her rookie season brought her and her contemporaries a significant milestone: She was the first woman golfer to earn $1 million for a single season.

A native of Ayr, Queensland, Australia, Webb began playing golf at the age of eight, when she competed in her first tournament. It was also her first time playing eighteen holes. Over the two days of the tournament, she shot 150 and 135, respectively. She also won her first trophy: The Encouragement Award. She seems to have gotten a little better since then.

As an amateur, Webb was the 1994 Australian Stroke Play champion. She represented Australia in international competition six times from 1992-94. Fellow countryman, Greg Norman, recognized her talent early on and arranged for personal, specialized coaching for her at his home in Florida. Webb turned pro in 1994 playing on the Futures Tour and the Women Professional Golfers' European Tour, where she earned Rookie of the Year honors in 1995. At the Australian Masters that year, she posted a second place finish behind Laura Davies. She also had her European LPGA Tour debut in 1995 where she posted a fourth place finish in Portugal. She got her first victory in only her fourth pro tournament.

Toward the end of the 1995 season, Webb announced her presence even before joining the LPGA Tour by winning the Weetabix Women's British Open with a 14-under 278, six strokes ahead of runners-up, American Jill McGill and perennial rival, Annika Sorenstam of Sweden. After that win, Webb joined the LPGA Tour in October 1995.

Webb kicked off her rookie year in 1996 with a second place finish at the season-opener, the Chrysler-Plymouth Tournament of Champions. But she didn't have long to wait for her first LPGA title. The very next week at the Health South Inaugural, Webb finished the final round in a three-way tie with Jane Geddes and Martha Nause at 7-under, and took the tournament on the fourth hole of a sudden-death playoff. Her third tournament brought another second place finish, one stroke behind Meg Mallon. She followed that performance with top ten finishes in the PING/Welch's Championship, the Standard Register PING, and the Nabisco Dinah Shore to lead the LPGA earnings list—only six events into her rookie season. It was promising to be a great year. After only a few weeks she'd already earned enough money to buy her first house in Orlando, Florida.

Webb captured the second title of her rookie season at the Sprint Titleholders Championship in Daytona Beach, Florida, including a second round 7-under 65. Her third title of the year came in September at the SAFECO Classic, with a two shot victory over Tammie Green. But it was her next win that would push Webb into the record books. At the season-closing ITT LPGA Tour Championship she shot 69-70-68-65 to win her fourth title of the 1996 season and made her the first woman golfer to win one million dollars in a single season, with $1,002,000. She was also the first rookie on either the LPGA or the PGA Tours to surpass the earnings milestone. Her four victories tie her with Se Ri Pak for the second-winningest rookie, behind Nancy Lopez who recorded nine titles in her first full season on Tour. In addition to winning the Rookie of the Year

BELOW: Karrie Webb celebrates after winning the U.S. Women's Open at the Pine Needles Lodge and Golf Club. With her victory she became the second woman golfer to cross the $7 million mark in career earnings (Annika Sorenstam was the first).

OPPOSITE: Karrie Webb kisses her trophy after winning the U.S. Women's Open at the Pine Needles Lodge and Golf Club in Southern Pines, North Carolina, on June 3, 2001.

honors, Webb was awarded the 1996 ESPY for Female Golfer of the Year.

The next year Webb picked up right where she had left off in her rookie season. In 1997, she again won the Weetabix Women's British Open and successfully defended her title at the SAFECO Classic, in addition to winning the Susan G. Komen International. That year she also won her first Vare Trophy for lowest season scoring average with a 70.00. She won the trophy again in 1999 with a record low average of 69.43, and has been trading off the award with rival Sorenstam virtually year by year.

Webb's career since then has been nothing but stellar. She won her first major at the du Maurier Classic in 1999, following that with the Nabisco Championship in 2000. She won back-to-back U.S. Open titles in 2000 and 2001, and became only the fifth woman to complete a career Grand Slam at the McDonald's LPGA Championship in 2001. She was also the youngest woman to complete the slam, doing so at the tender age of twenty-seven. And if that weren't enough, Webb also won a career slam in a record-breaking span from first major win to fourth major win. She did it in one year, ten months, and twenty-four days. That's the fastest anyone has done it — male or female. All this has already brought her golf immortality: 2005 marks her induction into the LPGA Hall of Fame.

Records are made to be broken. But records of "firsts" can never be broken. Karrie Webb's record of the first woman golfer to break the $1 million single season threshold will stand forever. The only questions to be answered yet are how much more Webb can do in her career. The sky seems to be the limit.

CHAPTER 3

Associations & Tournaments

ompetition is the lifeblood of any professional sport, and organization is a necessary precondition to create a context for it, and, in turn, to sustain it successfully and keep the game healthy. Rules, ethics, standards, and a code of honor (often unwritten but understood) exist as a way of holding everyone involved accountable for his actions. Once a healthy competitive context is clearly established, the spirit of adhering to a code that is fair and accepted by all makes the game even more challenging and fun.

OPPOSITE: European Ryder Cup players Miguel Angel Jimenez (standing) of Spain, and Padraig Harrington, of Ireland, study a putt on the 15th hole in September 1999 at The Country Club in Brookline, Massachusetts.

Today's competitive players owe a debt of gratitude to the first governing bodies of golf. The Royal and Ancient Golf Club of St. Andrews in Scotland, was the first, founded in 1754. The United States Golf Association, which came into being in 1894, became the other powerful golf association. Today, the two groups work together to protect the integrity of golf by instituting and maintaining the rules of play, providing course rating and handicap systems, setting and evaluating equipment standards, and funding environmental research. Although the two associations have not always agreed, they have always cooperated in the quest for the best possible game. Today, they hold a summit meeting every four years to review policies and rules. Other groups have joined in the quest, as well, setting standards and creating tournaments. In 1901, British golfers formed the Professional Golfers' Association of Great Britain, followed in 1916 by the Professional Golfers' Association of America, helping to elevate professionals to a more respected status. In 1944, the first women's organization was founded, a forerunner of the LPGA.

In 1924 the first official "Money List" was compiled. The first winner was Paul Runyan, who won six times and had sixteen top-ten finishes. While topping the Money List does not confer the same prestige as winning one of the four major championships, it is generally accepted as a reasonable gauge of a player's form over an entire season. Since 1981, the Money Leader has been presented with the Arnold Palmer Trophy.

The USPGA had begun a Hall of Fame in 1940, followed by the LPGA in 1950. The World Golf Hall of Fame opened in 1974 and incorporated the earlier organizations, plus numerous international groups, including the Royal Canadian Golf Association, the Australian PGA, and the R&A. With special categories including Lifetime Achievement, Veterans, and International, The World Golf Hall of Fame aims to honor all those individuals deserving of recognition through their contributions to the game.

With each association sponsoring one or more tournaments, they have created an international playing circuit that forms the context for golf today. This chapter will highlight the firsts in major championships around the world, as well as some of the more memorable moments in these matches.

The First American Amateur Association

The United States Golfing Association

1894

BELOW: Theodore A. Havemeyer, the USGA's first president, formed the first American Amateur Association.

OPPOSITE: Amateur golfer Bobby Jones of Atlanta, Georgia, follows through on his swing at the start of a nine-hole practice round, and his first ever shot in the Pacific coast, at Lakeside Country Club in Los Angeles, California, in August 1929.

The foundation of the United States Golf Association (USGA) was the end product of a December 22, 1894, meeting of delegates in New York City. They came from Newport Golf and Country Club (Rhode Island), St. Andrew's (Yonkers, New York), Shinnecock Hills (Southampton, New York), The Country Club (Brookline, Massachusetts), and the Chicago Golf Club. Theodore A. Havemeyer was elected the USGA's first president.

That meeting stemmed from a dispute over the question of a national amateur champion. In 1894, the Newport Golf and Country Club and the St. Andrew's Golf Club had vied for the finest amateur players to participate in their separate tournaments, each club intending to declare its own national champion.

Newport club member W.G. Lawrence bested a field of twenty to win the stroke-play tournament. St. Andrew's member Laurence Stoddart took down a field of twenty-seven in a match-play competition. Both clubs declared their winner national amateur champion. Charles Blair Macdonald, the runner-up in both tournaments, took the opportunity to press for a uniform set of rules and a national governing body to conduct national championships.

Macdonald's complaints were aired at a dinner party held at the Calumet Club in New York. Over glasses of Bordeaux and through the dark clouds of cigar smoke, Havemeyer, without dissension from any of the attendees, moved "that the Amateur Golf Association of the United States be, and hereby is, formed…."The fledgling Amateur Golf Association of the United States soon changed its name to the United States Golf Association, reflecting in its inclusiveness its intention to hold an Open championship, which would involve both amateur and professional players. Macdonald went on to win the first official U.S. Amateur championship, which was held in 1895 at Newport.

Dedicated to the promotion and preservation of golf (its motto is "For the good of the game"), the USGA is currently guided by an Executive Committee, which is the organization's policymaking board and represents more than nine thousand member clubs and courses. Thirty committees, made up of volunteers, augment the Executive Committee. All committee members donate their services and pay their own expenses.

Today, the USGA conducts thirteen national championships annually, and the number of players who enter grows at a terrific rate. The national championships are:

- United States Open
- United States Women's Open
- United States Senior Open
- United States Junior Amateur
- United States Girls' Junior Amateur
- United States Amateur Public Links
- United States Women's Amateur Public Links
- United States Amateur
- United States Women's Amateur
- United States Mid-Amateur
- United States Women's Mid-Amateur
- United States Senior Amateur
- United States Women's Senior Amateur

In cooperation with the Royal and Ancient Golf Club of St. Andrews, Scotland, the USGA conducts the Walker Cup, a biennial competition between teams of male amateur golfers, the United States versus Great Britain and Ireland. Since 1932, the USGA, with the British Ladies Golf Union, has held the Curtis Cup Match, played between teams of women amateur golfers. The USGA conducts both championships when they are played in this country.

In addition to the national championships, the USGA also oversees the process of interpreting and refining the rules (in cooperation with The Royal and Ancient); defines amateur status; runs the national handicapping system, known as the Golf Handicap and Information Network (GHIN); does research to improve golf course playing conditions and reduce water use; and maintains equipment standards.

A museum located at the USGA's headquarters in Far Hills, New Jersey, is dedicated to preserving the game's history.

The First British Open
Prestwick, Scotland

1860

OPPOSITE: "Young" Tom Morris, the first British Open winner, gets ready to swing as onlookers take in the action.

BELOW: American golfing icon Arnold Palmer waves to his fans on the Swilken Bridge on the Old Course at St. Andrews Golf Club in July 1995. The former Open Champion has announced that he no longer will compete in the British Open.

Golf's oldest and most exalted championship was first proposed at a meeting of the Prestwick Club in 1856, but it would be another four years before the inaugural tournament was played.

In 1860, eight professional players gathered outside the Red Lion Hotel in Prestwick, where the tournament rules were announced and the competitors had to sign off on them before they hit the links. Still, there was some doubt as to whether professionals, who were the only ones allowed to compete, could honor the rules set before them. The contest was held over the club's twelve holes, with three rounds being played on the same day starting at noon. The eventual winner was Willie Park from Musselburgh, with a total of 174.

What had undoubtedly enticed the participants to enter the tournament was the event's prize. In addition to a ten-pound purse, the club had commissioned a red leather belt (at a cost of twenty-five pounds) to present to the eventual winner. It became known simply as the "Championship Belt," and was awarded to the winner of the British Open until 1870, when Tom Morris, Jr., won the belt three times consecutively, which meant he was allowed to keep it. Without the belt, the club canceled the competition for a year. In 1872, the Claret Jug became the official trophy of the tournament. "Young" Tom Morris, as he was also known, won the first Claret Jug.

Until 1873, the Championship was always held in Prestwick. For one year it was moved to St. Andrews in Scotland. Thereafter, it was decided to hold the event on different courses in England and Scotland. By 1892, there were enough competitors that the contest was changed to 72 holes played over two days. In 1894, it was first played in England. The British Open was played for the first and only time outside England and Scotland in 1951, when it was held at Royal Portrush in Ireland.

From 1915 to 1920, and 1940 to 1946, the event was cancelled due to the world wars. The Open Championship has been contested every year since 1946.

Today, players qualify by playing on courses near the host club in the days preceding the event. With a purse of considerably more than ten pounds, the British Open is considered one of the most prestigious tournaments in golf.

The First U.S. Amateur Championship

Newport Golf and Country Club, Rhode Island

1895

BELOW: Teeing off in the final match of the first Amateur Golf Championship, held at St. Andrew's Golf Club in Yonkers, New York, in October 1894, is Charles B. MacDonald of the Chicago Golf Club. Waiting his turn is L.B. Stoddart, of Yonkers, who defeated MacDonald, one up. Looking on (at left) is John Reid, called the "Father of Golf in America."

The United States Golf Association began its first full year of operation in 1895, slating Amateur, Open, and Women's Amateur Championships for later that year. The Amateur and U.S. Open Championships were held during the same week of October at Newport Golf and Country Club.

The Amateur Championship is the oldest golf championship in the United States, just one day older than the U.S. Open. Except for an eight-year period, from 1965 to 1972, when it was stroke-play, the Amateur has been a match-play championship.

Over the years, as interest in the game grew and the number of quality players increased, it became necessary to establish a national handicapping system to determine who was eligible to compete in the Amateur. The USGA's first national handicap list, which was published for the 1912 Championship, was the precursor to the present-day USGA Golf Handicap System.

Throughout its history, the U.S. Amateur has been the most coveted of all amateur titles. Many of the great names of professional golf, such as Gene Littler, Arnold Palmer, Jack Nicklaus, Lanny Wadkins, Craig Stadler, Jerry Pate, Mark O'Meara, Hal Sutton, Phil Mickelson, and Tiger Woods, grace the Havemeyer Cup.

It was, however, longtime amateur Bobby Jones who first attracted media coverage and filled the galleries at the Amateur Championship. Jones captured the championship a record five times (1924, '25, '27, '28, '30). His 1930 victory capped a dazzling moment in golf history, when at Merion Cricket Club in Ardmore, Pennsylvania, Jones' victory clinched the Grand Slam, the four major American and British championships in one year.

The First Major Championship Decided by Sudden Death
PGA Championship

1977

This would have been the chance for the Golden Bear to set yet another benchmark and tie the great Walter Hagen for most PGA Championship victories with five. But Jack Nicklaus' opportunity to make history would be put on hold — he shot a disappointing 73 in the final round — as Lanny Wadkins took the first and only major of his career.

It did not come easily. It was at the 1977 USPGA Championship at Pebble Beach that Wadkins needed overtime to win the first major tournament decided by a sudden-death playoff. Extra frames between Lanny Wadkins and 1961 U.S. Open champion Gene Littler lasted just three holes.

Littler seemed to have had the title in the bag on the match's final day, but began to fade on the back nine. He bogeyed five of the first six holes, and was tied with Nicklaus for the lead, while Wadkins remained one stroke behind. Nicklaus bogeyed on the seventeenth, but Wadkins managed a birdie at Pebble Beach's famous eighteenth, tying with Littler for the lead.

Wadkins started the playoff by hitting his second shot into the deep rough. His next shot left was an eighteen-foot downhill putt that Wadkins drained. "I was stunned. He couldn't do it again with forty balls," Littler said. Both players birdied the next (a par 5) before Wadkins claimed the title by holing a six-foot (2m) par putt on the third.

A decade later, Wadkins was again involved in a sudden-death playoff. This time he was on the losing end. At the USPGA Championship at Palm Beach National, a bogey by Wadkins gave Larry Nelson the win.

Nicklaus did eventually equal Hagen's record, winning at Oak Hill in 1980.

The First U.S. Open Tournament
Newport Golf and Country Club

1895

BELOW: Horace Rawlins, winner of the first U.S. Open, is a picture of concentration as he follows his shot after working out of the rough.

OPPOSITE: Hale Irwin, the bespectacled thirty-four-year-old former Colorado football player, notched his second United States Open golf championship in 1979, when he won the event with an even par 284 for the seventy-two holes. Irwin hugs his caddy, Joe Foy, after winning the tournament.

The first U.S. Open tournament was held just one day after the first U.S. Amateur Championship, and as something of an afterthought. Both tournaments had originally been slotted for September but were postponed because of a conflict with the America's Cup yacht races, which were at the time a more revered sports spectacle in Newport.

Amateur golf was more prominent and prestigious than the professional game in those days. Players who were sponsored and played for money were considered less in keeping with the gentlemanly nature of the sport during that era.

The first tournament saw eleven players, ten of whom were professionals, tackle the 36-hole competition — four individual rounds of nine holes around the course — in one day. The $150 prize (the total purse being a whopping $335) went to Horace Rawlins, an English professional who happened to be an assistant pro at the Newport club. Rawlins also won a gold medal and the Open Championship Cup, which his club was allowed to keep and display for one year.

In its first decade, it was the British professionals, including Willie Anderson, who won in 1901 and then again for three years in a row starting in 1903, who dominated the U.S. Open. John J. McDermott became the first native-born American winner in 1911 and repeated as champion in 1912. When Francis Ouimet, a twenty-year-old American amateur, beat two well-known English professional players, Harry Vardon and Ted Ray, in a playoff in 1913, public interest began to build. Tickets were sold to the public for the first time in 1922. By the 1920s, Bobby Jones had come on the scene. He won the U.S. Open four times (1923, 1926, 1929, and 1930), permanently establishing American dominance in the tournament.

Professional players dominated from the start. The last amateur to win the U.S. Open was John Goodman in 1933. (The others were Ouimet in 1913, Jerome D. Travers in 1915, Charles Evans, Jr., in 1916, and of course, Jones in the 1920s.) Television coverage began in the 1950s, making the tournament accessible to a far wider range of spectators. Joining Anderson and Jones with four U.S. Open victories were Ben Hogan (1948, 1950, 1951, 1953) and Jack Nicklaus (1962, 1967, 1972, and 1980).

In 2002, the U.S. Open came to Bethpage, New York. It was the first time that the national championship was held on a public course — Bethpage State Park (The Black Course).

The First Professional Golfing Organization in the United States
Professional Golfers' Association of America

1916

The initial steps toward forming a professional association for golfers were taken on January 17, 1916, when Philadelphia department store heir Rodman Wanamaker hosted a luncheon at the Taplow Club in New York City. Wanamaker, who was a man of wide interests, invited a group of New York area golf professionals, along with several notable amateur golfers and other prominent golf enthusiasts, to discuss the possibility of forming a national organization for professional golfers. Its goals would be to spark interest in the game and bring attention to the role of the golf professional. Thirty-five people showed up, including Walter Hagen and course architect A.W. Tillinghast.

Wanamaker had noted a growing public fascination with the game, and he wanted to piggyback on that enthusiasm to create an organization through which golf professionals could prosper, and the interested public could participate. On April 10, 1916, the Professional Golfers' Association of America was formed. In setting down its constitution and bylaws, the eighty-two charter members of the PGA agreed, among other goals, to "Elevate the standards of the golf professional's vocation" and "Assist deserving unemployed members to obtain positions."

As part of the deal, Wanamaker offered to put up money for a tournament. The first PGA Championship was held in October 1916, at the Siwanoy Country Club in Bronxville, New York. Englishman Jim Barnes was the winner, taking home the first Wanamaker Trophy. The inaugural issue of *The Professional Golfer of America* appeared in May 1920. It was renamed *PGA Magazine* in 1977, and stands today as the United States' oldest golf publication. By 1925, membership in the PGA had grown to almost 1,500. Annual dues were $5. The PGA sponsored the first Ryder Cup Match in 1927. In 1933, the PGA elected its first U.S.-born president, George Jacobus, who had started his golf career as a caddy. In 1937, the PGA held its first Seniors' Championship.

By the mid-1960s, PGA membership had reached 6000. Over the years, as the PGA flourished and began to sponsor tournaments around the country, two kinds of professional golfers developed: club pros and touring pros. The touring professionals plied their trade from city to city, playing tournaments and exhibitions rather than sticking to one course or club. In 1968, the PGA tournament players formed a separate Tournament Players Division that was responsible for the tournament schedule — that group became the PGA Tour. The PGA remained the organization of the club professional. The PGA and the PGA Tour continue to be close allies.

In the last quarter of the century, the PGA began to seriously promote golf to the public, developing golfing history exhibits, promoting golf tourism, and expanding its professional education offerings. In an effort to develop the next generation of golfers, in 1976, the PGA held its first junior championship. Two years later, it established the PGA Junior Golf Foundation, to continue to promote and teach the game to young people.

By the new millennium, PGA membership had reached more than 30,000, including apprentices. Today, it is the largest working sports organization in the world. It conducts the Ryder Cup Matches, the PGA Championship, the Senior PGA Championship, and the PGA Grand Slam of Golf. Plus, it operates more than forty tournaments for PGA professionals, and holds the annual Buick Scramble, the world's largest golf tournament, with more than 100,000 participants.

THE PROFESSIONAL GOLFERS' ASSOCIATION CHAMPIONSHIP

1916

at Siwanoy C. C., Bronxville, N. Y.

Tom Kerrigan
C. G. Adams

George McLean
Tom McNamara
} Kerrigan
6 and 4

Alec Smith
James Ferguson
} McLean
6 and 5

} Kerrigan
2 and 1

Jim Barnes
George Fotheringham
} Smith
4 and 2

Willie Macfarlane
Robert McNulty
} Barnes
8 and 7

M. J. Brady
James West
} Macfarlane
10 and 9

} Barnes
8 and 7

} Barnes
3 and 1

Emmett French
Ed. Townes
} Brady
7 and 6

Bye
Jack Dowling
} French
3 and 1

} Macfarlane
3 and 2

J. J. O'Brien
Wilfred Reid
} Dowling

George Simpson
Walter Fovarque
} O'Brien
1 up

} Dowling
1 up (37)

} Macfarlane
2 and 1

} Barnes
6 and 5

Bob MacDonald
Jim Donaldson
} Simpson
6 and 5

Walter Hagen
J. R. Thomson
} MacDonald
3 and 2

} O'Brien
3 and 2

Jock Hutchison
Joe Mitchell
} Hagen
7 and 6

W. Brown
F. Clarkson
} Hutchison
11 and 9

} Hagen
3 and 2

} Hagen
10 and 9

Cyril Walker
L. Tellier
} Brown
Default

Jack Hobens
Mike Sherman
} Walker
4 and 2

} Hutchison
11 and 9

} Barnes
1 up

} Hobens
Default

} Walker
5 and 4

} Hutchison
4 and 3

} Hutchison
2 up

1917-1918—No Competition because of World War.

SIWANOY COUNTRY CLUB 1916
FIRST PGA CHAMPIONSHIP

The First Professional Golfing Organization in Great Britain

The Professional Golfers' Association of Great Britain

BISHOPGATE, LONDON

1901

Although professional golf had a firm hold in England well before the beginning of the twentieth century, tournaments were scarce. Most British pros were firmly club-based. In 1901, English pros got together to form the Professional Golfers' Association of Great Britain, with its first offices established in Bishopgate, London.

For most of Britain's golf professionals, the chance to play in a 36- or 54-hole stroke-play match, especially if it offered a cash prize, was a rare opportunity. Most pros were committed to the daily task of teaching amateurs at their clubs. And this was the way it stayed until well after World War II, despite the rise of the PGA Tour in the United States.

As the number of events slowly increased, the best club professionals started to devote more and more time to tournament play. Thus, the opportunity of earning a living from tournament golf alone became a distinct possibility, if only for a privileged few. Finally, just as in North America, two distinct types of golf professionals emerged—those who played tournaments and those who taught in the clubs. And to discern one from another was becoming easier and easier as time went on. It wasn't long before the tournament pros felt that the PGA of Great Britain was failing to look after their interests properly so a special Tournament Players' Division of the PGA was set up in 1971 under the guidance of John Jacobs.

In 1972, tournaments from Europe were included in the Order of Merit for the first time. At that time, the Order of Merit was given to the person who had the most points over a golf season. The higher up a player finished in an official OM tournament, the greater the number of points he received. Nowadays, the OM position is decided on money won in official events.

Up until the early 1970s, most tournaments in Europe were held in Britain, because most of the leading professionals were either British or Irish. Indeed, the word "European" wasn't actually used in the organization's title until 1977, when it became known as the PGA European Tournament Players' Division. In 1979, it became the PGA European Golf Tour.

Since 1981, the Tour's headquarters have been at Wentworth in Surrey, and in 1984 the Tour became a limited company. The club pros (PGA of Great Britain) now have their base at The Belfry in the Midlands.

The First Walker Cup Match
Southampton, New York

1922

BELOW: Great Britain/ Ireland Walker Cup team member Richard McEvoy hits from the trees on the 14th hole during Walker Cup play at Ocean Forest Golf Club on Sea Island, Georgia, in August 2001.

OPPOSITE: Opposing captains Bobby Jones (right), American captain of the American Walker Cup team, is shown being congratulated by Roger Wethered, Great Britain's captain, after the United States team was victorious during matches at Sandwich in Kent, England, in 1930.

The Walker Cup Match originated with a plan presented to the Executive Committee by George Herbert Walker, USGA president in 1920 (also grandfather and great-grand-father of the 41st and 43rd presidents of the United States). Walker had noted the public interest in two amateur matches between the United States and Canada that had taken place in 1919 and 1920. Shortly thereafter, the USGA Executive Committee had been invited to Great Britain for a series of sit-downs with the Royal and Ancient Golf Club of St. Andrews Rules Committee. The result was a proposed international match, featuring players from many different nations, to be called "The United States Golf Association International Challenge Trophy."

Things turned out a little differently. Although the USGA sent invitations to many countries, in the wake of World War I, none could afford to send a team. The press, meanwhile, dubbed the competition "the Walker Cup," a name that stuck. In the end, only the R&A (with a team representing Great Britain and Ireland) and the Americans played. Today the Walker Cup Match continues to be made up of one team from the United States and one team from England, Ireland, Scotland, and Wales. The teams consist of not more than ten players and a captain.

The first Walker Cup Match was held in 1922 at the National Golf Links of America in Southampton, New York. The United States team, led by Captain William C. Fownes, Jr. (who had put together the earlier U.S.-Canada matches), won the match 8 to 4 over the British team.

In 1924, the decision was made to meet every other year, which has been the case except during World War II. After the 1938 match at St. Andrews, Scotland, the competition was discontinued until 1947, when it resumed, again at St. Andrews, and ever since it has alternated between courses in the United States and Great Britain.

The Walker Cup matches have involved many of the most respected figures in golf history. Bobby Jones, one of the great amateur champions, was involved in five of the first six matches between 1922 and 1930. Jack Nicklaus, arguably the most successful player the game has ever seen, played in two matches. Francis Ouimet, Cyril Tolley, and Roger Wethered, all captains of the R&A, gave the Walker Cup early recognition. Bill Campbell, the only person to serve both as president of the USGA and captain of the R&A, played eight times between 1951 and 1975, the longest stretch of participation by any player. And more recently, Tiger Woods was able to include a match in his short but impressive tenure.

Although the U.S. teams have dominated the match from the beginning, the team from Great Britain and Ireland took the cup in 1999, then defended their championship in 2001— the first time in the history of the match they had been able to take back-to-back wins. Most participants agree, however, that regardless of which team wins, it is the spirit of international cooperation that makes the Walker Cup one of the greatest traditions in golf history.

The First PGA Championship

Bronxville, New York

1916

OPPOSITE: A recent scenic look at the Siwanoy Golf Course shows that it has ably withstood the test of time since the glory days of Jim Barnes.

Just a few months after the founding of the PGA in 1916, with Rodman Wanamaker having donated $2,580 for the purse, the first PGA Championship was held. The Siwanoy Country Club, in Bronxville, New York hosted.

James "Long Jim" Barnes, a native of Cornwall, England (who was actually a resident of Philadelphia), met Jock Hutchison, Sr., from St. Andrews, Scotland, in the finals. Barnes took the victory by just one stroke, becoming the first to have his name engraved on the Rodman Wanamaker Trophy.

World War I interrupted the event for the next two years, and it would be several more before an American-born PGA professional would claim the Championship. In 1919 Barnes captured his second consecutive Championship. He reached the finals again in 1921, but lost to Walter Hagen. Winning again in 1924, '25, '26 and '27, Hagen took a record-tying five PGA Championships. Gene Sarazen would claim victories in 1922, '23, and '33. Hagen and Sarazen faced each other in 1923 in what has been called "golf's greatest match," in which "The Squire" edged out "The Haig" with a birdie on the 38th hole.

Of the world's four principal golf championships, only the PGA was played during the World War II years (except for 1943), though the field was much reduced. Byron (also known as "Lord Byron") Nelson was defeated by one stroke by Henry Picard in 1939, but reached the finals in four of the next five PGA Championships, and took the Wanamaker Trophy twice, in 1940 and '45. Sam Snead won in 1942, triumphing again in 1949 and 1951, and came in third more than twenty years later, when he played the 1974 championship. Ben Hogan won in 1946 and again in 1948, the last PGA before his near-fatal car accident. In 1957, the PGA considered changing the format to a combination of medal- and match-play but, influenced by the advent of television broadcasting, opted for the stroke-play format, which began in 1958.

An amazing finale to a PGA Championship came in 1961 at Olympia Fields. On the last three greens of regulation play, 45-year-old Jerry Barber holed putts of 20 feet (6m) (birdie), 40 feet (12m) (par) and 60 feet (18.5m) (birdie) respectively to tie Don January, who had held a four-stroke lead with just three holes to play. Barber had nine single-putt greens in his final round of 70. He then won the following day's playoff, 67-68.

Jack Nicklaus won the first of his record-tying five in 1963. With his February 1971 victory, Nicklaus became the first professional to win the modern Grand Slam of golf for the second time. He would go on to win four PGA Championships in thirteen years, (the others were 1971, 1973, 1975, and 1980) including runner-up twice. He placed nine times in the top four, and won his fifth victory by a record margin of seven strokes.

Arnold Palmer set his own record with rounds of 68-68-69-69, but ultimately never took a Championship.

Of the fifteen playoffs in PGA history, perhaps the most exciting was the 2000 showdown between defending champ Tiger Woods and Bob May. Woods and May each finished with 31 on the back nine, tying for the lowest 72-hole score in relation to par (18-under-par 270) in Championship history. In the process, Woods became the first player since Ben Hogan in 1953 to win three major championships in one year. He also erased a PGA "jinx" by being the first to collect back-to-back Championships in the stroke-play era.

The First Ryder Cup Match

Worcester, Massachusetts

1927

To most golfers it's considered the fifth major. And though golfers don't receive any compensation for playing in the Ryder Cup, it is one of the most fiercely contested and revered team competitions in golf.

The idea came from Samuel Ryder, the son of a Manchester corn merchant, who became wealthy by selling seeds in envelopes. A golf enthusiast, he became distressed at the failure of British players to win the British Open in the face of challenges by Americans like Bobby Jones. He went so far as to sponsor a talented club pro named Abe Mitchell. Ryder approached the PGA with an offer to donate a trophy for an international match between the leading professionals from Great Britain and Ireland, and those of the United States.

In 1926, an informal match was played at Wentworth, Surrey. Britain and Ireland were represented by Abe Mitchell and George Duncan. The United States had Walter Hagen and Jim Barnes. To Ryder's delight, the British and Irish team won. A year later, the first official Ryder Cup match was staged at Massachusetts' Worcester Country Club. (Ryder carried his love for golf to the grave; he was buried with his mashie.)

Great Britain's original choice as captain, Abe Mitchell, was forced to withdraw from competition because of appendicitis before the team set sail from Southampton. Ted Ray assumed his duties. The two-day contest consisted of four foursomes and eight singles, each game played over 36 holes. (This format continued until 1961.)

The hosts led 3 to1 after the first day foursomes, and then romped through the singles 61/2-11/2. Great Britain and

Ireland's only victory in the singles came from George Duncan, who beat Joe Turnesa, one-up. Overall, the United States won nine matches that day. After that, the Ryder Cup was played every odd year, alternating between courses in Britain and the United States, except during World War II.

For fifty years, the match remained a contest between the United States and the Great Britain and Ireland teams. However, between 1935 and 1977, Great Britain and Ireland managed to manufacture only one victory in eighteen meetings. So, when the match was held in 1979, Great Britain and Ireland decided to also include golfers from continental Europe, with the expectation that the series would soon become competitive again. And, over the years, it certainly has.

In 1997, the Ryder Cup made its first trip to the continent, where the matches were staged in Sotogrande, Spain. Seve Ballesteros, a veteran of eight previous Ryder Cup Teams, guided a team featuring five rookies to victory over an American team that featured Masters Champion Tiger Woods, British Open Champion Justin Leonard, and PGA Champion Davis Love, III. At the Ryder Cup match in 1999, the United States team staged a sensational comeback. Facing a four-point deficit after two days of competition, on the final day of competition, the first six U.S. players went to work, winning an average of four holes per match, amassing twenty-three birdies against only three bogeys. Though the team won eight singles matches, it needed a crucial half-point

to win back the Cup for the first time since 1993. Justin Leonard, who trailed Spain's Jose Maria Olazabal by four holes with seven to play, came up big. He sank an uphill 45-foot (13.5m) birdie putt on the seventeenth green, triggering a raucous celebration by his team-mates. Once things quieted down, Olazabal barely missed his 25-foot (7.5m) uphill birdie putt, ending with a birdie on the eighteenth. It was not enough to prevent the Ryder Cup from changing hands.

Afterwards, U.S. Captain Ben Crenshaw put the win into its historical context: "We all know about Francis Ouimet and his [1913 U.S. Open] victory against two of the finest British players of his time. That's a little bit spooky. Justin made his putt on the same green Ouimet made his. And [Ouimet's] house is right across the street." The U.S. victory was the biggest comeback in Ryder Cup history; their singles win was the best final-day performance since 1979.

The 34th Ryder Cup matches were to be played from September 28 to 30, 2001, but in the aftermath of the World Trade Center tragedy on September 11 of that year, Ryder Cup officials decided to stage the matches in 2002 instead. PGA Chief Executive Officer Jim Awtrey explained the decision: "It was important to us that the Matches be played and not cancelled…. We will work with our counterparts in Europe over the next year to ensure that the 34th Ryder Cup Matches are played in the spirit in which they were meant." Officials announced that the Ryder Cup would thenceforward be played during even years.

The First Masters Tournament
Augusta, Georgia

1934

BELOW: Tiger Woods (left) receives the 2002 Masters green jacket from Augusta National Golf Club chairman William W. "Hootie" Johnson, Sunday, April 14, 2002, at the Augusta National Golf Club in Augusta, Georgia. Woods won his second consecutive title and third overall, with a 12-under-par 276.

OPPOSITE: Horton Smith, winner of the first Masters' Invitation Golf Tournament at Augusta, Georgia, in 1934, is congratulated on his victory by tournament co-creator Bobby Jones (left). Returning to competition after four years of inactivity, Jones finished out of the money in a tie for thirteenth place.

Unlike golf's three other major championships, which are run and controlled by national organizations, the U.S. Masters belongs solely to one club — Augusta National in Georgia. The club was the creation of two men: Bobby Jones, who retired from competition in 1930 after capturing the "old grand slam" (the U.S. Open, U.S. Amateur, British Open, and British Amateur) and Clifford Roberts, a Wall Street banker and an acquaintance of Jones.

Unlike most clubs, where the majority of members live and work in close proximity to the course, Augusta National, as the name suggests, was to draw its members from all over the United States. The only local members would be those brought in to help with the everyday administration and maintenance. (This membership policy lent Augusta National an exclusive character that has not always been to its benefit; it still has no female members.) The pair enlisted the services of Dr. Alister MacKenzie, a famous golf course architect who shared many of Jones' theories on course design, to create the layout, a task he started in the spring of 1931. A year later the club opened.

Among Jones' goals for the club was to stage an invitational tournament. Roberts wanted the event to be called the Masters Tournament; Jones, ever the understated, unassuming gentleman amateur golfer, objected, thinking the name pretentious. So, in 1934, the first Augusta National Invitational Tournament was played. Horton Smith captured the opener, beating Craig Wood by one stroke, 285-284. The seventy-two-strong field included Paul Ronyan, Billy Burke, Willie MacFarlane, Walter Hagen, and a host of other internationally known golf stars. Bobby Jones himself played, coming out of retirement and ending up in thirteenth place. Jones, who had played as an amateur throughout his career, insisted that amateurs be part of the Masters and that commercialization be avoided. To this day these traditions mark the Masters.

Horton Smith, who earned $1,500 for his winning effort, praised Jones' achievement. "There is nothing monotonous about that course and it is one of the most beautiful I ever played," Smith said. "Each one of the holes presents something new." Interestingly, for that first year only, what are now known as the front and back nines were played in reverse.

The next year's Masters saw Gene Sarazen hit the "shot heard 'round the world," when he holed a double eagle at the fifteenth to tie Craig Wood and force the Tournament's only 36-hole playoff. Sarazen won the extra hole.

The tournament's title remained unchanged until 1939, when Jones finally relented and the name was officially and permanently changed to the Masters. Starting in 1940, the tournament was set for the first week in April. In 1942, Byron Nelson defeated Ben Hogan 69 to 70 in an 18-hole playoff. The competition that year fielded only forty-two players, the smallest turnout in the history of the tournament. Eighty-eight players had been invited; World War II prevented more than half from attending. The next three tournaments were canceled, and cattle and turkeys were raised on the Augusta National grounds in aid of the war effort.

In 1950, Jimmy Demaret became the first player to win the Masters three times. Ben Hogan, coming back from a near-fatal car accident, took the 1951 Masters, then won again in 1953. In 1954 Sam Snead beat defending champion Hogan by just one stroke in a playoff for his third Masters. It earned him

$5,000, the largest payday to that time for a Masters champion. Arnold Palmer's 1958 win (his first major, and the first of his four Masters' championships) began the tradition of "Amen Corner." The part of the course where Rae's Creek meets the thirteenth fairway was so named by golf writer Herbert Wind when he traced Arnold's victory to that crucial sector.

In 1960 the Par 3 Contest began, won that year by Sam Snead (to this day, no Par 3 Contest winner has ever won the Masters the same year as his short-course victory). In 1961 South African Gary Player become the first foreign-born Masters champion. The first three-way playoff at the Masters occurred in 1962, when Palmer defeated Player and Dow Fisterwald. The year of Jack Nicklaus' first Masters triumph was 1963; Palmer's fourth came in 1964. In 1966 Nicklaus became the first Masters champion to defend his title successfully; 1968 was a heartbreaker for Roberto De Vincenzo, who inadvertently signed a scorecard with a fatal error.

In 1972, Nicklaus matched Palmer with a fourth Masters win, then exceeded it with a fifth in 1975. 1976 was the year Raymond Floyd matched Nicklaus' tournament record of 17-under 271. Player took his third Masters in 1978, shooting an 8-under 64 in the final round. In 1979, Fuzzy Zoeller defeated Ed Sneed in the first-ever sudden-death playoff at the Masters.

Seve Ballesteros won in 1980, just four days after his twenty-third birthday, while in 1986, aged forty-six, Jack Nicklaus

donned his sixth green jacket. That year also saw Nick Price set the course record with a 9-under 63. Bernhard Langer of Germany became the third foreign-born winner in 1985, followed by Scotsman Sandy Lyle in 1988, then Nick Faldo of England in 1989, who not only sank the longest putt in Masters history, but came back the next year to win again. The UK's streak continued in 1991, when Welshman Ian Woosnam won.

Despite a win by Fred Couples in 1992, American dominance of the Masters was definitely over. The 1990s saw wins by Spain's Jose Maria Olazabal (1994 and 1999), Langer (1993), and Faldo (1996). In 1997, Tiger Woods became the youngest-ever winner, and broke the Tournament four-day scoring record that had stood for thirty-two years.

The new millennium began with a win by the Philippines' Vijay Singh, followed by another Tiger Woods record-breaker in 2001, when Woods' Masters victory made him the first player in history to take four majors in succession and the first million-dollar money-winner ever at the Masters.

In 2002, Augusta National Chairman Hootie Johnson announced changes to the venerable course, and that year's players found alterations to nine holes, with some 300 feet (9m) total added length. Tiger Woods, for the second consecutive year, outshone his competitors to take the 2002 Masters. The changes, though controversial, could never undermine a course as well made as Augusta National.

The First Women's Golf Association in the United States
WPGA

BELOW: Babe Zaharias, one of the original founders of the Ladies Professional Golf Association, plays for $5,000 in prizes in the thirteenth annual Los Angeles Open Golf Tournament in 1938. Zaharias, an all-around athlete, matched her skills against the men, driving on the tournament course.

OPPOSITE: Eight founders of the Ladies Professional Golf Association pose at a celebration of the association's 50th anniversary in October 1999, in New York. Pictured here (left rear) are Marilyn Smith, Marlene Hagge, Alice Bauer, Louise Suggs, and Betty Jameson; (front row) Bettye Sanoff, Shirley Spork, and Patty Berg.

The first U.S. golf association for women wasn't a rousing success by any stretch, but it did establish the promise of something greater and more long-lasting. The women behind the association were three talented, take-charge players: Hope Seignious, Betty Hicks, and Ellen Griffin. In 1944, they stepped up and officially started the Women's Professional Golf Association (WPGA).

Of course, women had been playing golf for years, but it was not until after World War II that barriers to their participation in sports began to fall, and women's professional golf really took off. The WPGA was not financially sturdy and never fully got off the ground, but during its five-year tenure, it accomplished three important tasks. First, since the women players had suffered from exclusionary policies themselves, they rejected the "Caucasians only" rule that marred the constitutions of so many other organizations (the PGA, for example, did not drop it until 1961). Second, the WPGA founded the Women's National Open Tournament, and finally, it laid the groundwork for the next women's golf association, which would be much more successful.

In 1946, the WPGA held the first Women's Open at the Spokane Country Club, bringing together the "big four" names in women's golf at the time — Patty Berg, Louise Suggs, Betty Jameson, and Mildred "Babe" Didrikson Zaharias. The WPGA ran the Women's Open for three more years.

In 1949, as the WPGA was failing, golf's pre-eminent women decided to form a new organization. The twelve founders who created what came to be called the Ladies Professional Golf Association were Alice Bauer, Patty Berg, Bettye Danoff, Helen Dettweiler, Marlene Bauer Hagge, Opal Hill, Betty Jameson, Sally Sessions, Marilynn Smith, Shirley Spork, Louise Suggs, and Babe Zaharias. Fred Corcoran, Babe's business manager, became the LPGA's first tournament manager. Since there was as yet no money for staff, the golfers did the rest of the work of organizing and promoting the tour themselves.

In 1950, the LPGA conducted fourteen events that offered nearly $50,000 in prize money. Those early LPGA events often featured mostly amateur players, as the numbers of professional women golfers remained low. The first official LPGA tournament, the 1950 Tampa Open, was won by an amateur named Polly Riley. In 1952, Jameson instituted the Vare Trophy, which goes to the player with the lowest season scoring average. Named in honor of amateur great Glenna Collett Vare, the first trophy went to Berg in 1953.

With the exhaustive efforts of the league's founders, the LPGA began to gain momentum. Working with a women's clothing manufacturer, Corcoran helped create a series of four 36-hole tournaments known as The Weathervane. The tournaments were played across the country, and each one was worth $3,000. The Weathervane was the

backbone of the early tour. By 1959, the LPGA Tour had twenty-six tournament stops and played for $200,000.

The 1960s put the LPGA on firm ground. New talent and friendly rivalries — in particular that of Mickey Wright and Kathy Whitworth — made for good television. The color barrier was broken by Althea Gibson (see page 71) in 1963, followed by Renee Powell in 1967. New awards, Rookie of the Year and Player of the Year, allowed the LPGA to laud its greatest talents. By the end of the decade, the tour was up to thirty-four events and $600,000 in prize money.

The 1970s saw a new generation of players take the stage, with star performances from such names as JoAnne Carner, Judy Rankin, Jan Stephenson, Jane Blalock, and Amy Alcott. Through the decade, Carner won 23 of her 43 career victories, Rankin took 25 tournament titles, Blalock won 24 events, and Stephenson triumphed at 16, including three major championships. Alcott joined the Tour in 1975, captured her first tournament title in her third event, and established the winner's tradition of diving into the pond at the eighteenth green at the Colgate Dinah Shore, now known as The Nabisco Championship.

Nancy Lopez dominated the tour from the late 1970s through the '80s. In her first year, she swept the field to be named Rookie of the Year, Player of the Year, and winner of the Vare Trophy. She won 48 tournaments, entering the LPGA Tour Hall of Fame in 1987. Lopez shared the LPGA Tour of the 1980s with such talented players as Pat Bradley, Betsy King, Beth Daniel, Patty Sheehan, and Juli Inkster.

In the 1990s women's prize money finally caught up, and the LPGA closed the decade at a high of some $36 million. The tour also became more international, with such talented new players as Annika Sorenstam (Sweden), Karrie Webb (Australia), and Se Ri Pak (Korea), grabbing the attention of the golf community and giving such U.S. players as Dottie Pepper, Michelle McGann, Donna Andrews, Brandie Burton, Meg Mallon, and Kelly Robbins some tough competition. The Solheim Cup (named for Karsten Solheim, inventor of the first investment-cast, heel- and toe-weighted club), which was introduced in 1990, makes the rivalry official every two years.

By the early 2000s, it was clear that the LPGA had done much more than fulfill the dreams of its founders. As women's golf had grown so dramatically in popularity, so had the LPGA become a pre-eminent sports organization, supporting and encouraging women golfers to take their place in the golfing pantheon.

The First Celebrity Tournament
Bing Crosby's Clambake

1937

The gathering started out informally and innocuously but in no time at all it became a big hit with "the boys." In the summer of 1934, Bing Crosby — an avid and skilled amateur golfer — first invited several of his golfing buddies to spend a weekend with him in North Lake Tahoe to play in an unofficial tournament at the Old Brockway Golf Course at King's Beach.

The get-together was a smash with everyone, and all agreed that it should be an annual event that invited golf stars and Hollywood stars alike to take the opportunity to play against each other over a challenging course just for fun — and, of course, to see who might win.

In 1937, Crosby chose the Rancho Santa Fe near San Diego as the tournament's first official venue. Officially named the Bing Crosby Pro-Amateur Tournament, but known to all as "Crosby's Clambake," the tournament required the golfers to go a full eighteen holes for a purse containing $3,000. Some of the amateurs included Zeppo Marx, Guy Kibbee, and Fred Astaire. Bob Gardner, an amateur from Los Angeles, reflecting on the relaxed attitude at "Bing's thing," said: "Everything was pretty informal at the 'The Crosby' in those days. Our entry fee was three bucks, and if they missed you one day, they would catch you the next." The legendary Sam Snead won the first tournament, and true to his "hillbilly" reputation, when he saw the winner's check coming his way, he said, "If you don't mind, Mr. Crosby, I'd rather have cash."

The final Crosby "clambake," which also included steaks and whatever else they could find to throw on the grill, was played at Rancho Santa Fe in 1942. The tournament was cancelled for the duration of World War II. It resumed in 1947 on the scenic Monterey Peninsula's storied Pebble Beach course, where it was held each February through the rest of Crosby's life.

Good weather could never be guaranteed in February, and the frequency with which inclement conditions plagued the tournament led to the nickname "Crosby weather." In 1960, it rained so hard that Johnny Weissmuller declared, "I've never been so wet in my life." Known for his movie role as Tarzan, Weissmuller had previously won Olympic gold as a champion swimmer. At the 1962 tournament, golf pro Jimmy Demaret awoke to a snow-covered course and said, famously, "I know I got loaded last night, but how did I end up in Squaw Valley?" (a ski resort in California). And in 1998, the tournament became perhaps the longest PGA event ever played: the final round was held six months after the tournament began because El Niño-powered rain washed out Sunday's play. Phil Mickelson eventually won the tournament.

Beginning in 1958, the Crosby was broadcast nationally, and frequently ranked as the most-viewed golfing event of the year. One exception was 1974, when Crosby was gravely ill in the hospital. After Crosby's death, his widow was pressed to change the name of the tournament to the AT&T Bing Crosby golf tournament. She refused, and withdrew the Crosby name from the tournament. The tournament that helped Crosby raise millions for various charities is now called the AT&T National Pro-Am.

The First Women's U.S. Open
Spokane Country Club

1946

The U.S. Women's Open is the oldest championship open to women professionals and amateurs. The first Women's U.S. Open was played under the auspices of the short-lived Women's Professional Golfers Association. In 1946, the WPGA unveiled the Women's Open, the only tournament that was a match-play event, at the Spokane (Washington) Country Club. (Ironically, the event was funded by a men's organization called the Spokane Athletic Round Table, which contributed the $19,700 purse from the proceeds of its slot machines.)

Patty Berg won the first championship by defeating Betty Jameson, 5 and 4, in the 36-hole final. (Berg went on to be the WPGA's leading player, with three victories in each of 1948 and 1949, and holds an LPGA record of fifteen major championship titles.) Over the tournament's first four years, each of women's golf "Big Four" was a winner: Betty Jameson came back to win the 1947 match, followed by Babe Zaharias in 1948, and Louise Suggs in 1949.

The WPGA ran the championship for three years, until it disbanded. In 1950, the Ladies Professional Golf Association was founded, with Berg as president, and took over the Women's U.S. Open. Babe Zaharias won the 1950 Women's Open, followed by Betsy Rawls in 1951, and Louise Suggs in 1952. In 1953, the LPGA asked the USGA to take over management of the championship. The first USGA Women's Open was played at the Country Club of Rochester, New York, with a field of thirty-seven. Betsy Rawls took the championship, the second of her four Women's Open titles (her others came in 1957 and 1960). Rawls' greatest rival during that period was Mickey Wright, who also won four times (1958, 1959, 1961, 1964), the only other woman to rack up that many Opens. Babe won again in 1954, after recovering from an operation for the cancer that eventually killed her.

In 1965, reflecting the growing popularity of women's golf, the final round of the championship was televised nationally for the first time. The Women's Open has been televised ever since, with all four rounds now broadcast. By 1970, the field had grown to 131 and the prize money totaled almost $35,000; that year Donna Caponi became the second player to successfully defend a championship. In 1976, JoAnn Carner beat Sandra Palmer in a playoff. In 1979, Jerilyn Britz defeated Debbie Massey and Sandra Palmer, the 1975 Champion, with a score of 284, even par, the lowest 72-hole total since the USGA assumed sponsorship of the Open in 1953. The next year, winner Amy Alcott broke that record with a 280. More than three hundred entries were received, and prize money had reached a record $140,000.

By the late 1980s, the U.S. Women's Open had truly become a great international contest. Until then, there were just three foreign-born winners: Fay Crocker of Uruguay (1955), Catherine Lacoste of France (1967), and Jan Stephenson of Australia (1983). In 1987, England's Laura Davies triumphed over Ayako Okamoto by two strokes and JoAnne Carner by three strokes in an eighteen-hole playoff. In 1995, Patty Berg, Louise Suggs, Betsy Rawls, and twenty-two other past champs came to celebrate the fiftieth anniversary of the Open, and watch Annika Sorenstam of Sweden become the thirteenth player to make the Women's Open her first professional victory in the United States. The others were Kathy (Baker) Guadagnino in 1985, Jan Geddes in 1986, Laura Davies in 1987, and rookie Liselotte Neumann in 1988. Sorenstam's second victory, in 1996, saw her establish the incredible new 72-hole scoring record of 272, 8 under par. In 1998, twenty-year-old Se Ri Pack of South Korea, in an impressive match, bested amateur Jenny Chuasiriporn of Maryland to become the youngest-ever Women's Open champion. It was her second consecutive victory in a women's major. In 2000 and 2001, Australian Karrie Webb won back-to-back Opens, and became, along with Annika Sorenstam, one of two players in LPGA history to earn $1 million in four separate seasons.

The First African-American to Win a PGA Tour Event

Pete Brown

1964

When the notorious "Caucasian Clause" was finally removed from the PGA constitution in 1961, it became possible for minority-member golfers, several of whom had played exclusively in Negro Leagues, to secure a Professional Golfers Association card.

Pete Brown was not the first African-American to obtain a player's card; that barrier was broken by Charlie Sifford, a contemporary of his. Brown's achievement was to become the first African-American to win a PGA event, the 1964 Waco Turner Open.

Brown played on the PGA tour for seventeen years, during which he won a second tour victory (the Andy Williams Open in San Diego, California, in 1970). Brown was also the victor at numerous other non-PGA events, including the National Negro Championship, which he won four consecutive times.

Brown and Sifford and other African-American golfers of their era, all of whom simply wanted a fair shot to compete in the game they loved in an equitable way, had to endure gross indignities — and sometimes even outright cruelty — just to play on the same course or to be acknowledged in the eyes of their white counterparts.

As these courageous African-American golfers continued to seek acknowledgment and fair treatment, however, there were occasionally some lighter moments. For example, Bill Spiller, a top African-American golfer who was among the first to legally challenge the Tour's racist rules, crashed a country club dance after the Bakersfield Open. Dressed in coat and tie, he walked right to the head table in the clubhouse, where blacks were not allowed, and asked the wife of the club president to dance. She obliged, and the two of them took a whirl around the floor.

Brown, Sifford, and Spiller, and later Lee Elder, are just a few of the African-American golfers who fought for their right to play the game; and though the efforts of many other courageous players before and after them may have gone unremarked, it was their combined perseverance that made it possible for golfers of all backgrounds to play today.

The First Nationwide Live Telecast Golf Tournament

Tam O'Shanter World Championship

1953

ABOVE: Lew Worsham (second left) holds the trophy that he won at Tam O'Shanter Country Club, in 1953. Frank Stranahan was the winner in the men's Amateur Division. Tops in the Women's Professional Division is Patty Berg (second right) and winner in the women's amateur division is Margaret "Wiffi" Smith.

OPPOSITE: Golf promoter George May takes a practice drive on the 18th hole at the Tam O'Shanter Country Club in Niles, Illinois, in 1958.

For the American Broadcasting Company, the allure was the event's prize money. The network was just getting its footing in the early 1950s. And during that same period, televisions were cropping up in households around the country, as the new technology began to phase out the radio as the medium of choice.

Network executives reasoned that if they took a booming sport such as golf, with its telegenic greens and country club aesthetic, and put those images on television, it would be a perfect recipe for a nationally televised event.

Still, in order to make this come off ABC needed a cash cow. Along came George S. May, who owned the Tam O'Shanter Country Club in Chicago, a place where he staged golf tournaments for professionals in the early 1940s. May's purse money for the pros, in particular the men, was always very generous — far outpacing other offerings of that time. By 1953, the purse had grown to $25,000 for the winner's share alone, which was more than the total take for every other tournament on the pro circuit.

ABC caught wind of that beneficence, which prompted the network to air the event, provided that May put up the money for the coverage himself. May complied because he recognized the publicity value inherent in the medium. So, in July 1953, ABC broadcast the very first nationwide, live telecast of a golf tournament, the Tam O'Shanter World Championship.

With about twenty minutes of airtime left, only one golfer had any chance of catching leader Chandler Harper, who was already in the clubhouse. One camera, placed high up on a grandstand behind the eighteenth green, zeroed in on Lew

Worsham, winner of a playoff against Sam Snead for the 1947 U.S. Open (the first local live telecast of a golf tournament). Worsham needed a birdie 3 to tie Harper and had a shot of roughly 115 yards (103m) to a green that was just beyond a creek. He picked a wedge, took a swing, and sent the ball on a line toward the green. Astoundingly, it landed on the front of the putting surface, then ran some 45 feet (13.5m) dead into the hole for an eagle 2. The shot gave Worsham a one-shot victory over Harper, and the $25,000 first prize. It gave ABC a spectacular broadcast. The Nielsen rating indicated that more than one million people saw Worsham's wedge shot, the largest-ever simutaneous audience for a golfing event.

So enthused by the theatrics of the event's waning moments, May eagerly announced the following year's top prize would be doubled to $50,000 — an inordinate payout for 1953. That generosity not only gave professionals an incentive to return to Tam O'Shanter, but it also stoked the public's interest to a higher level.

ABC was not slow to recognize the potential for drawing in viewers, and in the latter part of the decade began to air a series called "All-Star Golf." The show matched two professional golfers against each other each week, with the ultimate winner taking home a prize of $80,000. NBC followed up with its own show, "World Championship Golf." The connection between golf and television had been firmly established.

The First Skins Game
Palmer, Player, Nicklaus, Watson

1983

What began as a bet on fur pelts has evolved into one of the most lucrative and spirited competitions in the game of golf. Although no one knows for sure, it seems to have started centuries ago in seaport towns like St. Andrews, where fur traders made regular stops. At St. Andrews, instead of going straight into the harbor, the traders would anchor offshore and row in to play the eleven holes over the Old Course from the sea to the town. They would often play against the furriers to whom they were planning to sell their pelts, and to spice things up the merchants would bet a specific number of fur skins on each hole.

Today, a "skin" is a hole won by a golfer in competition against three other golfers. Each hole is assigned a dollar value at the start. The game is played hole by hole. If a hole is tied, the players move on to the next hole, but the amount for the previous hole is added to the next. Over the centuries, the basic concept of the game has remained the same, with cash payouts replacing fur skins and fur traders supplanted by amateur golfers and touring professionals.

The first official pro Skins Game was played on Thanksgiving Weekend in 1983. The idea came from television executives Don Ohlmeyer and Barry Frank, who believed that a televised game played in the skins format, featuring the top players and generous payouts, would attract a substantial television viewership. They convinced the power-packed foursome of Jack Nicklaus, Arnold Palmer, Gary Player, and Tom Watson to participate. Those first skin payoffs were $10,000 each for the first six holes, $20,000 each for the next six, and $30,000 each for the final six for a total purse of $360,000. Player captured the inaugural match, which was an unqualified success. The Skins Game has been played every year since, and has spun off an LPGA and a Senior Tour version.

The first Senior Skins Game was played in 1988; Chichi Rodriguez took the $40,000 purse. In 2000, The Senior Skins recreated the original 1983 competition; once again, Player was triumphant.

By 2001, the game's purses had increased considerably. In the nineteenth annual Skins Game, which was played at the Landmark Golf Club in Indio, California, each of the first six holes was worth $25,000; the next six, $50,000; holes thirteen to seventeen, $70,000; and the eighteenth hole, $200,000. 2001's foursome included Tiger Woods, Greg Norman, Jesper Parnevik and defending champion Colin Montgomerie. For the first time in the history of the competition, players were required to post the lowest score on back-to-back holes or tie for the lowest score in order to win the skin. Otherwise, the skin was carried over. The only time that rule did not apply was at the eighteenth hole. Norman wound up taking the entire $800,000 prize as he sank a 15-foot (4.5m) birdie putt on the game's last day.

The First Tour for Senior Players
The PGA Senior Tour

1980

There were plenty of special events for senior players, including The Legends of Golf and the venerable PGA Seniors' Championship, but by the late 1970s, these events were not enough to sate the growing number of older players' need for gainful competition. Simply put, the over-fifty crowd craved more play on a consistent basis, and wanted a tour designed to suit their interests.

A number of senior players, some of whom were coming to the tail end of their careers on the PGA Tour, began discussions with the PGA brass in 1979, and soon the makings of a new Tour were coming into view. A landmark meeting on January 16, 1980, laid the formal groundwork for the Senior PGA Tour; notable golfers in attendance were Sam Snead, Gardner Dickinson, Bob Goalby, Don January, and the late Dan Sikes and Julius Boro — all leaders on the All-Time Money List.

They decided that longevity and recognition alone would not be enough to entitle a senior golfer to a player's card on the newly formed circuit. Eligibility criteria would hinge on a player's total career victories and position on the All-Time Money List. They also chose a tour format emphasizing pro-am play. A field of 50 players (later expanded to 52) was set, so that two rounds of pro-am play could be held, and one of those pro-am rounds could be made an official round of the tournament.

The next step was to establish events for Senior Tour play. The Senior PGA Championship had been established back in 1937, and had a storied history. Two new tournaments were conducted in 1980, one in Atlantic City, New Jersey (won by Don January) and the other in Melbourne, Florida (won by Charlie Sifford).

The Senior Tour grew progressively over the next few years, with five events in 1981, eleven in 1982, and eighteen tournaments by 1983. Prize money surpassed $3 million for the 1983 season. Fellow Texans Miller Barber and Don January emerged as the dominant players, each taking two money titles in the first four years of the Senior Tour, and between them winning forty-one events. Among the other notable performers on the new circuit during that stretch was Arnold Palmer, who won the 1980 U.S. Senior Open.

By the mid-eighties, the Senior Tour had expanded to almost thirty tournaments worth more than $5 million in prize money. These, unheard of during the first heyday of most senior tour members, prompted Don January to state, "If you'd have told me back in 1980 that we'd have this many events and be playing for this much money, I'd have said you were crazy." In 1985 PGA Tour officials acknowledged the Senior Tour as a separate division of the PGA Tour. Television came calling, too, and ESPN aired seven events that year.

The 1990s marked the reunion of Lee Trevino and Jack Nicklaus with already-on-the-senior-tour players Arnold Palmer and Gary Player. Trevino wasted little time getting down to business, winning seven times in his first year. His official earnings of $1,190,518 not only made him the Tour's first "million-dollar man," but also the year's leading money-winner in all of golf. Others soon joined him in the seven-figure category. By 2002, Hale Irwin was dominating the Senior Tour, with thirty-four victories.

The Senior Tour has proven to be a great draw, bringing together the esteemed elder statesmen of golf.

The First Celebrated Upset of a Leader Going into a Major's Final Round

Greg Norman

1996

BELOW: Ever the gentleman, Norman (left), who folded miserably in the waning moments of the tournament, shakes hands with winner Nick Faldo, the eventual winner of the 1996 U.S. Masters.

OPPOSITE: Australia's Greg Norman collapses in heartache after narrowly missing his chip shot on the fifteenth green during the final round of the 1996 U.S. Masters Golf Championship at the Augusta National Golf Club in Augusta, Georgia.

When it has come to bagging the big one in his career, "The Shark" has had no bite. Aussie Greg Norman, nicknamed the "Great White Shark," has been one of the most hardluck golfers in the history of the game. He has eighteen PGA Tour victories, plus an impressive list of international triumphs, but only two majors to his name — the 1986 and 1993 British Opens — and none won in the United States.

Nowhere has that distinction been more pronounced than at the Masters, in which he has finished in the top six eight times without winning. His trials started in the 1986 Masters when he was up a stroke on Jack Nicklaus, who closed with a 65, entering the final hole. Norman needed only to make par on the eighteenth to force a playoff with Nicklaus. It was over when he hit his four-iron approach into the gallery well right of the green.

Later that year, at the PGA Championship at Inverness, Norman's troubles persisted. He was four up on the field going into Sunday's final round. Bob Tway mounted one of the greatest comebacks in recent history when he made up a nine-stroke deficit on Norman over the final two rounds. Tway covered the last thirty-six holes in eight-under par (64-70), to Norman's three-over (69-76), to win the tournament by two strokes.

In the 1987 Masters, Norman fell short again, at the hands of Larry Mize. Three players, including Mize, Norman, and former champion Seve Ballesteros, were locked in a playoff battle. Ballesteros three-putted on the first extra hole (the tenth) for a bogey five, missing his second putt from five feet (1.5m). At the second (eleventh), Mize pushed his approach shot off the green to the right, about forty yards (36m) from the cup, while Norman's ball landed on the fringe, forty feet (12m) from the hole. Mize then floored Norman by chipping in a birdie from a very precarious angle. Norman, needing to sink his birdie putt to move the playoff into a third extra hole, never came close to making it, leaving Mize the first Augusta-born player to win the Masters.

Almost a decade later, at the 1996 Masters, Norman was ranked number one in the world, and in a position to redeem himself at Augusta. And once more, he would snatch defeat from certain victory. He went into the back nine well in the lead, and with everyone believing the green jacket would be his, but Faldo erased a six-stroke deficit as Norman came undone and shot a 6-over-par 78, finishing second at 7-under with 281. Faldo had the day's best round, a 5-under 67, and finished with a 72-hole total of 12-under, 276. "We had an amazing day today," Faldo said. "I honestly feel for Greg and what he's going through. I hope it's remembered for my 67 and storming through. Unfortunately, it will probably be remembered for what happened to Greg."

By the early 2000s, back and hip problems were affecting Norman's play, and it seemed the major championship would never be his. Augusta National gave him a special invitation to play in the 2002 Masters, the first time in ten years that Norman had needed such an invitation, which Augusta typically reserves for international players.

Despite his problems with the Masters, Norman remains one of the top players on the career money list. His business, Great White Shark Enterprises, includes golf course design, turf, residential development, clothing, golf equipment distribution (it is the exclusive Titleist distributor in Australia), restaurants, wine-making, and yachts. In the end, by any measure, Norman has been one of the world's outstanding players.

The First Public Facility To Host a Major

Bethpage State Park (The Black Course)

FARMINGDALE, NEW YORK

2002

OPPOSITE: Phil Mickelson works out of the bunker on the sixth hole during the final round of the U.S. Open Golf Championship at the Black Course of Bethpage State Park in Farmingdale, New York, on June 16, 2002.

BELOW: Tiger Woods tees off the first hole during the final round of the U.S. Open Golf Championship at the Black Course of Bethpage State Park.

Even before the famed and treacherous Black Course at Bethpage was being readied for the best 156 golfers in the world, it was being hailed as "The People's Open." That's because for the first time in the history of the sport, a major tournament, the U.S. Open, came to a course where the average Joe could play a round for $31 and not have to be a member of a club.

The decision by the USGA to stage one of golf's Grand Slam events at a public venue underscored the governing body's sensitivity and awareness to the history of the game itself. Golf wasn't only open to the rich, it was also a game where the masses had a chance to compete against those who came from country clubs or the elite crowd.

Bringing the 102nd U.S. Open to Bethpage State Park, the largest public golf facility in the world, had a tremendous impact in underscoring public golf and giving public golf courses the recognition they deserve. And now, the casual and fanatical golfer alike can say, "I played where Tiger did."

The Black Course was opened in 1936. Many think it epitomizes U.S. golf course design. It was ranked the fourth best public course in the country by *Golf Magazine* in 1998. The Black Course is set at 7,214 yards (6,596.5m) and plays to par 35-35-70. It is the longest course in U.S. Open history, one yard longer than the Congressional Country Club course played for the 1997 Open. With its extended fairways and impossible rough, the Black Course is an extremely demanding course. There is even a sign at the first tee that says, "The Black Course is an extremely difficult golf course and is recommended only for the experienced player."

It was on that course that Woods, the only player under par (3-under 277), captured his second U.S. Open title and eighth USGA championship, tying him with idol Jack Nicklaus and leaving him one shy of Bobby Jones. Phil Mickelson, still seeking his first major, made a late dash to upend Woods but fell three strokes short, finishing even par overall.

On the last day, Mickelson, gave back his birdie at the first hole after suffering back-to-back bogeys at five and six. Still, he got the crowd roaring with a birdie at 8 and another drop-in birdie at 11. Then he two-putted 13 for another birdie and suddenly it appeared as if Mickelson might have a chance to win the Open on his 32nd birthday. But Mickelson then bogeyed 16 when his drive found the left rough and he three-putted 17 to drop back to even par.

It seemed fitting that the first U.S. Open to be held on a publicly-held course would be won by someone who grew up playing municipal golf. Woods cultivated his craft at a small course in Long Beach, California, and developed into the world's best player. He's the only golfer to win three straight U.S. Junior Amateurs and three consecutive U.S. Amateurs.

World Golf Hall of Fame Members

Inducted through Former Golf Hall of Fame

1974	Patty Berg, Walter Hagen, Ben Hogan, Robert T. Jones, Jr., Byron Nelson, Jack Nicklaus, Francis Ouimet, Arnold Palmer, Gary Player, Gene Sarazen, Sam Snead, Harry Vardon, Babe Zaharias.
1975	Willie Anderson, Fred Corcoran, Joseph C. Dey, Chick Evans, Tom Morris, Jr., John H. Taylor, Glenna C. Vare, Joyce Wethered
1976	Tommy Armour, James Braid, Tom Morris, Sr., Jerome Travers, Mickey Wright
1977	Bobby Locke, John Ball, Herb Graffis, Donald Ross
1978	Billy Casper, Harold Hilton, Dorothy Campbell Hurd Howe, Bing Crosby, Clifford Roberts
1979	Louise Suggs, Walter Travis
1980	Lawson Little, Henry Cotton
1981	Lee Trevino, Ralph Guldahl
1982	Julius Boros, Kathy Whitworth
1983	Bob Hope, Jimmy Demaret
1985	JoAnne Carner
1986	Cary Middlecoff
1987	Robert Trent Jones, Sr., Betsy Rawls
1988	Tom Watson, Peter Thomson, Bob Harlow
1989	Ray Floyd, Nancy Lopez, Roberto DeVicenzo, Jim Barnes
1990	William C. Campbell, Paul Runyan, Gene Littler, Horton Smith
1992	Hale Irwin, Chi Chi Rodriguez, Richard Tufts, Harry Cooper

Inducted via the LPGA Hall of Fame

1951	Betty Jameson
1977	Sandra Haynie, Carol Mann
1991	Pat Bradley
1994	Dinah Shore
1995	Betsy King
1999	Amy Alcott, Beth Daniel
2000	Juli Inkster
2003	Annika Sorenstam
2005	Karrie Webb

Elected through the Veterans Category

2000	Judy Rankin
2001	Donna Caponi

Elected through the PGA TOUR Hall of Fame

1996	Johnny Miller (inducted May 18, 1998)
1999	Lloyd Mangrum
2001	Greg Norman, Payne Stewart

Elected through the International Ballot

1997	Nick Faldo, Severiano Ballesteros (inducted March 22, 1999)

Elected through the Veterans Category

2000	Jack Burke, Jr.
2001	Allen Robertson

Elected through the Lifetime Achievement Category

2000	Deane Beman, Sir Michael Bonallack, Neil Coles, John Jacobs
2001	Judy Bell, Karsten Solheim

Masters Tournament Records

Year	Winner	Score	Year	Winner	Score
2002	Tiger Woods	70-69-66-71 = 276	1967	Gay Brewer, Jr.	73-68-72-67=280
2001	Tiger Woods	70-66-68-68 = 272	1966	Jack Nicklaus	68-76-72-72=288*
2000	Vijay Singh	72-67-70-69 = 278	1965	Jack Nicklaus	67-71-64-69=271
1999	Jose Maria Olazabal	70-66-73-71=280	1964	Arnold Palmer	69-68-69-70=276
1998	Mark O'Meara	74-70-68-67=279	1963	Jack Nicklaus	74-66-74-72=286
1997	Tiger Woods	70-66-65-69=270	1962	Arnold Palmer	70-66-69-75=280*
1996	Nick Faldo	69-67-73-67=276	1961	Gary Player	69-68-69-74=280
1995	Ben Crenshaw	70-67-69-68=274	1960	Arnold Palmer	67-73-72-70=282
1994	Jose Maria Olazabal	74-67-67-69=279	1959	Art Wall, Jr.	73-74-71-66=284
1993	Bernhard Langer	68-70-69-70=277	1958	Arnold Palmer	70-73-68-73=284
1992	Fred Couples	69-67-69-70=275	1957	Doug Ford	72-73-72-66=283
1991	Ian Woosnam	72-66-67-72=277	1956	Jack Burke, Jr.	72-71-75-71=289
1990	Nick Faldo	71-72-66-69=278*	1955	Cary Middlecoff	72-65-72-70=279
1989	Nick Faldo	68-73-77-65=283*	1954	Sam Snead	74-73-70-72=289*
1988	Sandy Lyle	71-67-72-71=281	1953	Ben Hogan	70-69-66-69=274
1987	Larry Mize	70-72-72-71=285*	1952	Sam Snead	70-67-77-72=286
1986	Jack Nicklaus	74-71-69-65=279	1951	Ben Hogan	70-72-70-67=280
1985	Bernhard Langer	72-74-68-68=282	1950	Jimmy Demaret	70-72-72-69=283
1984	Ben Crenshaw	67-72-70-68=277	1949	Sam Snead	73-75-67-67=282
1983	Seve Ballesteros	68-70-73-69=280	1948	Claude Harmon	70-70-69-70=279
1982	Craig Stadler	75-69-67-73=284*	1947	Jimmy Demaret	69-71-70-71=281
1981	Tom Watson	71-68-70-71=280	1946	Herman Keiser	69-68-71-74=282
1980	Seve Ballesteros	66-69-68-72=275	1945	No tournament	
1979	Fuzzy Zoeller	70-71-69-70=280*	1944	No tournament	
1978	Gary Player	72-72-69-64=277	1943	No tournament	
1977	Tom Watson	70-69-70-67=276	1942	Byron Nelson	68-67-72-73=280*
1976	Raymond Floyd	65-66-70-70=271	1941	Craig Wood	66-71-71-72=280
1975	Jack Nicklaus	68-67-73-68=276	1940	Jimmy Demaret	67-72-70-71=280
1974	Gary Player	71-71-66-70=278	1939	Ralph Guldahl	72-68-70-69=279
1973	Tommy Aaron	68-73-74-68=283	1938	Henry Picard	71-72-72-70=285
1972	Jack Nicklaus	68-71-73-74=286	1937	Byron Nelson	66-72-75-70=283
1971	Charles Coody	66-73-70-70=279	1936	Horton Smith	74-71-68-72=285
1970	Billy Casper	72-68-68-71=279*	1935	Gene Sarazen	68-71-73-70=282*
1969	George Archer	67-73-69-72=281	1934	Horton Smith	70-72-70-72=284
1968	Bob Goalby	70-70-71-66=277			

* Won tournament in playoff

British Open Champions

Year	Winner	Venue	Total	Year	Winner	Venue	Total
2001	David Duval	Royal Lytham & St. Annes	274	1986	Greg Norman	Turnberry Golf Links	280
2000	Tiger Woods	St. Andrews	269	1985	Sandy Lyle	Royal St George's	282
1999	Paul Lawrie	Carnoustie	290	1984	Seve Ballesteros	St. Andrews	276
1998	Mark O'Meara	Royal Birkdale	280	1983	Tom Watson	Royal Birkdale	275
1997	Justin Leonard	Royal Troon Golf Club	272	1982	Tom Watson	Royal Troon Golf Club	284
1996	Tom Lehman	Royal Lytham & St. Annes	271	1981	Bill Rogers	Royal St. George's	276
1995	John Daly	St. Andrews	282	1980	Tom Watson	Muirfield	271
1994	Nick Price	Turnberry Golf Links	268	1979	Seve Ballesteros	Royal Lytham & St. Annes	283
1993	Greg Norman	Royal St. George's	267	1978	Jack Nicklaus	St. Andrews	281
1992	Nick Faldo	Muirfield	272	1977	Tom Watson	Turnberry Golf Links	268
1991	Ian Baker-Finch	Royal Birkdale	272	1976	Johnny Miller	Royal Birkdale	279
1990	Nick Faldo	St. Andrews	270	1975	Tom Watson	Carnoustie	279
1989	Mark Calcavecchia	Royal Troon Golf Club	275	1974	Gary Player	Royal Lytham & St. Annes	282
1988	Seve Ballesteros	Royal Lytham & St. Annes	273	1973	Tom Weiskopf	Royal Troon Golf Club	276
1987	Nick Faldo	Muirfield	279	1972	Lee Trevino	Muirfield	278

Year	Winner	Venue	Score		Year	Winner	Venue	Score
1971	Lee Trevino	Royal Birkdale	278		1915	Not Held Due to World War I		
1970	Jack Nicklaus	St. Andrews	283		1914	Harry Vardon	Prestwick	306
1969	Tony Jacklin	Royal Lytham & St. Annes	280		1913	John H. Taylor	Hoylake	304
1968	Gary Player	Carnoustie	289		1912	Edward Ray	Muirfield	295
1967	Roberto DeVicenzo	Hoylake	278		1911	Harry Vardon	Royal St. George's	303
1966	Jack Nicklaus	Muirfield	282		1910	James Braid	St. Andrews	299
1965	Peter Thomson	Southport	285		1909	John H. Taylor	Deal	295
1964	Tony Lema	St. Andrews	279		1908	James Braid	Prestwick	291
1963	Bob Charles	Royal Lytham & St. Annes	277		1907	Arnaud Massey	Hoylake	312
1962	Arnold Palmer	Troon Golf Club	276		1906	James Braid	Muirfield	300
1961	Arnold Palmer	Birkdale	284		1905	James Braid	St. Andrews	318
1960	Kel Nagle	St. Andrews	278		1904	Jack White	Royal St. George's	296
1959	Gary Player	Muirfield	284		1903	Harry Vardon	Prestwick	300
1958	Peter Thomson	Royal Lytham & St. Annes	278		1902	Alexander Herd	Hoylake	307
1957	Bobby Locke	St. Andrews	279		1901	James Braid	Muirfield	309
1956	Peter Thomson	Hoylake	286		1900	John H. Taylor	St. Andrews	309
1955	Peter Thomson	St. Andrews	281		1899	Harry Vardon	Royal St. George's	310
1954	Peter Thomson	Royal Birkdale	283		1898	Harry Vardon	Prestwick	307
1953	Ben Hogan	Carnoustie	282		1897	Harold Hilton	Hoylake	314
1952	Bobby Locke	Royal Lytham & St. Annes	287		1896	Harry Vardon	Muirfield	316
1951	Max Faulkner	Royal Portrush	285		1895	John H. Taylor	St. Andrews	322
1950	Bobby Locke	Royal Troon Golf Club	279		1894	John H. Taylor	Royal St. George's	326
1949	Bobby Locke	Royal St. George's	283		1893	William Auchterlonie	Prestwick	322
1948	Henry Cotton	Muirfield	294		1892	Harold Hilton	Muirfield	305
1947	Fred Daly	Hoylake	293		1891	Hugh Kirkaldy	St. Andrews	166
1946	Sam Snead	St. Andrews	290		1890	John Ball	Prestwick	164
1945	Not Held Due to World War II				1889	Willie Park, Jr.	Musselburgh	155
1944	Not Held Due to World War II				1888	Jack Burns	St. Andrews	171
1943	Not Held Due to World War II				1887	Willie Park, Jr.	Prestwick	161
1942	Not Held Due to World War II				1886	David Brown	Musselburgh	157
1941	Not Held Due to World War II				1885	Bob Martin	St. Andrews	171
1940	Not Held Due to World War II				1884	Jack Simpson	Prestwick	160
1939	R Burton	St. Andrews	290		1883	Willie Fernie	Musselburgh	159
1938	R.A. Whitcombe	Royal St. George's	295		1882	Robert Ferguson	St. Andrews	171
1937	Henry Cotton	Carnoustie	290		1881	Robert Ferguson	Prestwick	170
1936	Alfred Padgham	Hoylake	287		1880	Robert Ferguson	Musselburgh	162
1935	Alfred Perry	Muirfield	283		1879	Jaime Anderson	St. Andrew's	169
1934	Henry Cotton	Royal St. George's	283		1878	Jaime Anderson	Prestwick	157
1933	Densmore Shute	St. Andrews	292		1877	Jaime Anderson	Musselburgh	160
1932	Gene Sarazen	Prince's	283		1876	Bob Martin	St. Andrews	176
1931	Tommy Armour	Carnoustie	296		1875	Willie Park	Prestwick	166
1930	Bobby Jones	Hoylake	291		1874	Mungo Park	Musselburgh	159
1929	Walter Hagen	Muirfield	292		1873	Tom Kidd	St. Andrews	179
1928	Walter Hagen	Royal St. George's	292		1872	Tom Morris, Jr.	Prestwick	166
1927	Bobby Jones	St. Andrews	285		1871	Not Held		
1926	Bobby Jones	Royal Lytham & St. Annes	291		1870	Tom Morris, Jr.	Prestwick	
1925	Jim Barnes	Prestwick	300		1869	Tom Morris, Jr.	Prestwick	
1924	Walter Hagen	Hoylake	301		1868	Tom Morris, Jr.	Prestwick	
1923	Arthur Havers	Royal Troon Golf Club	295		1867	Tom Morris, Sr.	Prestwick	170
1922	Walter Hagen	Royal St. George's	300		1866	Willie Park	Prestwick	169
1921	Jock Hutchinson	St. Andrews	296		1865	Andrew Strath	Prestwick	162
1920	George Duncan	Deal	303		1864	Tom Morris, Sr.	Prestwick	160
1919	Not Held Due to World War I				1863	Willie Park	Prestwick	168
1918	Not Held Due to World War I				1862	Tom Morris, Sr.	Prestwick	163
1917	Not Held Due to World War I				1861	Tom Morris, Sr.	Prestwick	163
1916	Not Held Due to World War I				1860	Willie Park	Prestwick	174

U.S. Open Records

Age

Oldest Champion
Hale Irwin in 1990: 45 years, 15 days
Raymond Floyd in1986: 43 years, 9 months, 11 days
Ted Ray in 1920: 43 years, 4 months, 16 days

Oldest to make cut
Sam Snead in 1973: 61
Jack Nicklaus in 1998: 58
Sam Snead in 1969: 57
Dutch Harrison in 1967: 57
Jack Nicklaus in 1997: 57

Youngest Champion
John J. McDermott in 1911: 19/10/14

Youngest Competitor
Tyrell Garth in 1941: 14

Champions

Most Victories
Willie Anderson: 4 (1901, 1903, 1904, 1905)
Robert T. Jones, Jr.: 4 (1923, 1926, 1929, 1930)
Ben Hogan: 4 (1948, 1950, 1951, 1953)
Jack Nicklaus: 4 (1962, 1967, 1972, 1980)
Hale Irwin: 3 (1974, 1979, 1990)

Consecutive Victories
Willie Anderson: 3 (1903, 1904, 1905)
John J. McDermott: 2 (1911, 1912)
Robert T. Jones, Jr.: 2 (1929, 1930)
Ralph Guldahl: 2 (1937, 1938)
Ben Hogan: 2 (1950, 1951)
Curtis Strange: 2 (1988, 1989)

Other Multiple Champions
Alex Smith: 2 (1906, 1910)
John J, McDermott: 2 (1911, 1912)
Walter Hagen: 2 (1914, 1919)
Gene Sarazen: 2 (1922, 1932)
Ralph Guldahl: 2 (1937, 1938)
Cary Middlecoff: 2 (1949, 1956)
Julius Boros: 2 (1952, 1963)
Billy Casper: 2 (1959, 1966)
Lee Trevino: 2 (1969, 1971)
Andy North: 2 (1978, 1985)
Curtis Strange: 2 (1988, 1989)
Ernie Els: 2 (1994, 1997)
Lee Janzen: 2 (1993, 1998)
Payne Stewart: 2 (1991, 1999)

Runner-up Finishes
Robert T. Jones, Jr.: 4 (1922, 1924, 1925, 1928)
Sam Snead: 4 (1937, 1947, 1949, 1953)
Arnold Palmer: 4 (1962, 1963, 1966, 1967)
Jack Nicklaus: 4 (1960, 1968, 1971, 1982)
Alex Smith: 3 (1898, 1901, 1905)
Tom McNamara: 3 (1909, 1912, 1915)

Top-Five Finishes
Willie Anderson: 11
Jack Nicklaus: 11
Alex Smith: 10
Walter Hagen: 10
Ben Hogan: 10
Arnold Palmer: 10
Robert T. Jones, Jr.: 9
Gene Sarazen: 9
Julius Boros: 9

Top-Ten Finishes
Jack Nicklaus: 18
Walter Hagen: 16
Ben Hogan: 15
Gene Sarazen: 14
Arnold Palmer: 13
Sam Snead: 12
Willie Anderson: 11
Alex Smith: 11
Julius Boros: 11
Robert T. Jones, Jr.: 10

The Last Time It Happened

Last foreign winner
Ernie Els, South Africa in 1997

Last to defend title successfully
Curtis Strange in 1989

Last to win three consecutive Opens
Willie Anderson in 1903-05

Last winner who won the Open on his first try
Francis Ouimet in 1913

Last winner to win the Open on his second try
Jerry Pate, T-18th in first in 1975, winner in 1976

Last amateur to win Open
John Goodman in 1933

Last start-to-finish winner (no ties)
Tiger Woods in 2000

Last winner to win money title in same year
Tiger Woods in 2000

Last winner to birdie the 72nd hole
Lee Janzen in 1993

Last winner to birdie the 72nd hole to force a playoff
Hale Irwin, in 1990

Last winner to birdie the 72nd hole to win by one stroke
Robert T. Jones, Jr. in 1926

Last winner to birdie the 72nd hole to win by two strokes
Lee Janzen in 1993

Last to win without a round in the 60s
Tom Kite in 1992

Last to win with all rounds in the 60s
Lee Janzen in 1993

Last to win with a round in the 80s
80, John McDermott, in playoff in 1911

Last to win with a round of 77
Sam Parks, Jr., in first round in 1935

Last to win with a round of 76
Johnny Miller, in third round in1973

Last to win with a round of 75
Payne Stewart, in playoff in 1991

Last to win after being in sectional qualifying
Steve Jones in 1996

Last to win after being in local and sectional qualifying
Orville Moody in 1969

Last winner between age 20-29
Tiger Woods was 24 in 2000

Last winner between age 30-39
Lee Janzen was 33 in 1998

Last winner over age 40
Tom Kite was 42 in 1992

Last winner who received a special exemption
Hale Irwin in 1990

Last defending champion to miss the cut
Ernie Els in 1995

PGA Championship Records

Age

Oldest Winner
Julius Boros in 1968: 48 years, 4 months, 18 days

Youngest Winner
Gene Sarazen in 1922: 20 years, 5 months, 22 days

Most Victories
Walter Hagen: 5 (1921, 1924, 1925, 1926, 1927)
Jack Nicklaus: 5 (1963, 1971, 1973, 1975, 1980)

Consecutive Victories
Walter Hagen: 4 (1924, 1925, 1926, 1927)

Most Runner-ups
Jack Nicklaus: 4 (1964, 1965, 1974, 1983)

Scoring *(Stroke Play, 1958 to present)*
Low 72 Holes: Steve Elkington in 1995 with 267 (68-67-68-64) and Colin Montgomerie
    in 1995 with 267 (68-67-67-65)
Lowest Score Under Par, 72 Holes: Steve Elkington in 1995 with 17-under; Colin Montgomerie
    in 1995 with 17-under
Low 72 Holes (non-winner): Colin Montgomerie in 1995 with 267
Highest 72-Hole Score by Winner: Larry Nelson in 1987 with 287
Low First 54 Holes: Ernie Els in 1995 with197, (66-65-66)
Low Last 54 Holes: Steve Elkington in 1995 with 199 (67-68-64), Colin Montgomerie in 1995
    with 199 (67-67-65)
Low First 36 Holes: Hal Sutton, 131, (65-66) in 1983; Vijay Singh, 131 (68-63) in 1993; Ernie Els,
    131 (66-65) in 1995; Mark O'Meara, 131 (64-67) in 1995
Low Last 36 Holes: Miller Barber, 132 (64-68) in 1969; Steve Elkington, 132 (68-64) in 1995;
    Colin Montgomerie, 132 (67-65) in 1995; Davis Love, III, 132 (66-66) in 1997; Bob May,
    132 (66-66) in 2000
Low Score, First Round: Ray Floyd with 63 in 1982; Michael Bradley with 63 in 1995
Low Score, Second Round: Bruce Crampton with 63 in 1975; Gary Player with 63 in 1984;
    Vijay Singh with 63 in 1993
Low Score, Third Round: Miller Barber with 64 in 1969; Hal Sutton with 64 in 1984; Bob Tway
    with 64 in 1986; Jay Haas with 64 in 1995
Low Score, Fourth Round : Brad Faxon with 63 in 1995
Low Score, 9 Holes: Brad Faxon with 28 (front nine, final round) in 1995
Largest Winning Margin: Jack Nicklaus, 7 shots in 1980
Most Rounds in the 60s: Jack Nicklaus in 41
Most Sub-par Rounds : Jack Nicklaus in 52
Lowest Scoring Average (Min. 30 rounds): Steve Elkington, 70.57 with 42 rounds

Miscellaneous
Most Appearances: Arnold Palmer – 37
Most Cuts Made: Ray Floyd: 27, Jack Nicklaus – 27
Most Rounds Played: Jack Nicklaus – 126
Most Top Three Finishes: Jack Nicklaus – 12
Most Top Five Finishes: Jack Nicklaus – 14
Most Top 10 Finishes: Jack Nicklaus – 15
Most Top 25 Finishes: Jack Nicklaus – 23
Wire-to-Wire Winners: Bobby Nichols, 1964; Ray Floyd, 1969; Jack Nicklaus, 1971;
    Ray Floyd, 1982; Hal Sutton, 1983.

Ryder Cup Records

USA	Europe
Highest Margin of Victory	
1967 in Houston, Texas: 23.5 to 8.5	1985 in Sutton Coldfield, England: 16.5 to 11.5
Most Times on Ryder Cup Team	
Lanny Wadkins: 8 (1977,79,83,85,87,89,91,93)	Nick Faldo: 11 (1977,79,81,83,85,87,89,91,93,95,97)
Ray Floyd: 8 (1969,75,77,81,83,85,91,93)	Christy O' Connor, Sr.: 10 (1955,57,59,61,63,65,67,69,
Billy Casper: 8 (1961,63,65,67,69,71,73,75)	71,73)
Youngest Player	
Horton Smith in 1929: 21 years, 4 days	Sergio Garcia in 1999: 19 years, 8 months, 15 days
Oldest Player	
Raymond Floyd in 1993: 51 years, 20 days	Ted Ray in 1927: 50 years, 2 months, 5 days
Most Matches Played	
Billy Casper: 37	Nick Faldo: 46
Most Points Won	
Billy Casper: 23.5	Nick Faldo: 25
Arnold Palmer: 23	Seve Ballesteros: 22.5
Lanny Wadkins: 21.5	Bernhard Langer: 20.5
Most Singles Matches	
Arnold Palmer: 11	Neil Coles: 15
Most Foursome Matches	
Lanny Wadkins: 15	Nick Faldo: 18
Billy Casper: 15	Bernhard Langer: 16
Most Four-Ball Matches	
Billy Casper: 12	Seve Ballesteros: 15
Lanny Wadkins: 11	Bernhard Langer: 14
Raymond Floyd: 11	
Most Matches Won	
Arnold Palmer: 22	Nick Faldo: 23
Billy Casper: 20	Seve Ballesteros: 20
Lanny Wadkins: 20	Bernhard Langer: 18
Most Single Matches Won	
Arnold Palmer: 6	Peter Oosterhuis: 6
Billy Casper: 6	
Lee Trevino: 6	
Sam Snead: 6	
Most Foursome Matches Won	
Arnold Palmer: 9	Seve Ballesteros: 10
Lanny Wadkins: 9	Nick Faldo: 10
	Bernhard Langer: 10

Most Four-Ball Matches Won
Lanny Wadkins: 7
Arnold Palmer: 7

Ian Woosnam: 10
Seve Ballesteros: 8
Nick Faldo: 7

Most Matches Lost
Ray Floyd: 16

Christy O'Connor, Sr.: 21
Neil Coles: 21

Most Single Matches Lost
Ray Floyd: 4
Jack Nicklaus: 4

Christy O'Connor, Sr.: 10

Most Foursome Matches Lost
Ray Floyd: 8

Bernard Hunt: 9

Most Four-Ball Matches Lost
Curtis Strange: 5

Nick Faldo: 9

Teams With Most Ryder Cup Wins

European Team
Seve Ballesteros/Jose Maria Olazabal
Peter Alliss/Christy O'Connor

11 Wins, 2 Losses, 2 Halves (15 matches)
5 Wins, 6 Losses, 1 Halve (12 matches)

U.S. Team
Tom Kite/Curtis Strange
Larry Nelson/Lanny Wadkins

2 Wins, 3 Losses, 1 Halve (6 matches)
4 Wins, 2 Losses (6 matches)

Undefeated and Untied in 2 or more Matches
Jimmy Demaret: 6 wins
Billy Maxwell: 4 wins
Ben Hogan, Billy Burke & Johnny Golden: 3 wins

Paul Broadhurst, John Jacobs: 2 wins

Walker Cup Records

Age

Oldest Player
Hon. Michael Scott (GB&I) in 1934: 55 years, 8 months
William Hyndman (U.S.) in 1971: 55 years, 5 months
William C. Campbell (U.S.) in 1975: 52 years, 23 days

Youngest Player
Justin Rose (GB&I) in 1997: 17 years, 10 days
Ronan Rafferty (GB&I) in 1981: 17 years, 7 months
Peter Baker (GB&I) in 1985: 17 years, 10 months

Competitions

Most Times Competed for Great Britain & Ireland
Joseph B. Carr: 11 (1947, 1949, 1951, 1953, 1955, 1957, 1959, 1961, 1963, 1965, 1967)
Michael Bonallack: 9 (1957, 1959, 1961, 1963, 1965, 1967, 1969, 1971, 1973)

Most Times Competed for United States
Jay Sigel: 9 (1977, 1979, 1981, 1983, 1985, 1987, 1989, 1991, 1993)
Francis Ouimet: 8 (1922, 1923, 1924, 1926, 1928, 1930, 1932, 1934)
William C. Campbell: 8 (1951, 1953, 1955, 1957, 1965, 1967, 1971, 1975)
Jess W. Sweetser: 6 (1922, 1923, 1924, 1926, 1928, 1932)
Charles Coe: 6 (1949, 1951, 1953, 1959, 1961, 1963)

Most Years Between U.S. Selections
William C. Campbell: 24 (1951 and 1975)
Jack Westland: 21 (1932 and 1953)
Charles Kocsis: 19 (1938 and 1957)

Match Play

Largest Winning Margin, Singles *(18-Hole Match)*
9 and 7-Scott Hoch (U.S.) d. James Buckley, Honourable Company of Edinburgh Golfers, Muirfield, Scotland, 1979
8 and 7-Doug Clarke (U.S.) d. John Davies, Honourable Company of Edinburgh Golfers, Muirfield, Scotland, 1979
7 and 6-Scott Simpson (U.S.) d. Gordon Murray, Shinnecock Hills G.C., Southampton, N.Y., 1977
7 and 5-Robert Gamez (U.S.) d. Jim Milligan, Peachtree G.C., Atlanta, Ga., 1989
7 and 5-Joseph B. Carr (GB&I) d. R. H. Sikes, Ailsa Course, Turnberry, Scotland, 1963
7 and 5-Jodie Mudd (U.S.) d. Colin Dalgleish, Cypress Point Club, Pebble Beach, Calif., 1981

Largest Winning Margin, Singles *(36-Hole Match)*
13 and 12-Robert T. Jones, Jr. (U.S.) d. T. Philip Perkins, Chicago G.C., Wheaton, Ill., 1928
12 and 11-E. Marvin H. Ward (U.S.) d. J.J.F. Pennick, St. Andrews (Old Course), 1938
12 and 11-Robert T. Jones, Jr. (U.S.) d. Cyril J. H. Tolley, St. Andrews (Old Course), Scotland, 1926
11 and 10-Watts Gunn (U.S.) d. Ronald Hardman, Chicago G.C., Wheaton, Ill., 1928

Largest Winning Margin, Foursomes *(18-Hole Match)*
7 and 6-Bob Lewis, Jr., and Jim Holtgrieve (U.S.) d. Malcolm Lewis and Martin Thompson, Royal Liverpool G.C., Hoylake, England, 1983
7 and 5-Marvin Giles III, and Gary Koch (U.S.) d. Rodney Foster and Trevor Homer, The Country Club (Championship Course), Brookline, Mass., 1973

Largest Winning Margin, Foursomes *(36-Hole Match)*
9 and 8-E. Harvie Ward, Jr., and Jack Westland (U.S.) d. John D. A. Langley and Arthur H. Perowne, Kittansett Club, Marion, Mass., 1953
9 and 8-William J. Patton and Charles R. Coe (U.S.) d. Michael F. Bonallack and Arthur H. Perowne, Honourable Company of Edinburgh Golfers, Muirfield, Scotland, 1959

Highest Winning Percentage, Singles *(minimum four matches)*
1.000-John Harris, U.S. (6-0-0)
1.000-Robert T. Jones, Jr., U.S. (5-0-0)
.938-William C. Campbell, U.S. (7-0-1)
.875-Phil Mickelson U.S. (3-0-1)
.800-Ronnie White, GBI (4-1-0)

.750-Deane Beman, U.S. (4-1-1)
.750-Robert A. Gardner, U.S. (3-1-0)
.750-Jim Holtgrieve, U.S. (3-1-0)
.750-Allen Miller, U.S. (3-1-0)
.750-Philip Walton, GBI (3-1-0)
.750-Alan Brodie, GBI (3-1-0)

Highest Winning Percentage, Foursomes *(minimum four matches)*
1.000-Max R. Marston, U.S. (4-0-0)
.857-William J. Patton, U.S. (6-1-0)
.833-Jess W. Sweetser, U.S. (5-1-0)
.800-Robert T. Jones, Jr., U.S. (4-1-0)
.800-John Harris, U.S. (4-1-0)

Most Victories, Combined Play
Jay Sigel (U.S.): 18 (1977, 1979, 1981, 1983, 1985, 1987, 1989, 1991, 1993)
William C. Campbell (U.S.): 11 (1951, 1953, 1955, 1957, 1965, 1967, 1971, 1975)
William J. Patton (U.S.): 11 (1955, 1957, 1959, 1963, 1965)
John Harris (U.S.): 10 (1993, 1995, 1997)
Bob Lewis, Jr. (U.S.): 10 (1981, 1983, 1985, 1987)
Robert T. Jones, Jr. (U.S.): 9 (1922, 1924, 1926, 1928, 1930)
Francis Ouimet (U.S.): 9 (1922, 1923, 1924, 1926, 1928, 1930, 1932, 1934)

Most U.S. Matches Played, Combined
Jay Sigel: 33 (18-10-5)
William C. Campbell: 18 (11-4-3)
Francis Ouimet: 16 (9-5-2)
Marvin Giles III: 15 (8-2-5)
William J. Patton: 14 (11-3)
Bob Lewis, Jr.: 14 (10-4)
John Harris: 11 (10-1)

Undefeated in U.S. Singles Matches *(minimum four matches)*
6-0-John Harris
5-0-Robert T. Jones, Jr.
7-0-1-William C. Campbell
3-0-1-Phil Mickelson

Undefeated in U.S. Foursomes Matches *(minimum four matches)*
4-0-Max R. Marston

Undefeated in U.S. Foursomes and Singles Matches *(minimum four matches)*
5-0-Donald Cherry (2-0, 3-0)
4-0-Brad Elder (2-0, 2-0)

Miscellaneous

Most Times Site of Walker Cup
St. Andrews (Old Course), Scotland: 8 (1923, 1926, 1934, 1938, 1947, 1955, 1971, 1975)
Royal St. George's G.C., Sandwich, England: 2 (1930, 1967)
The Country Club, Brookline, Mass.: 2 (1932, 1973)
Honourable Company of Edinburgh Golfers, Muirfield, Scotland: 2 (1959, 1979)
Pine Valley G.C., N.J.: 2 (1936, 1985)

Largest Winning Margin, Team
14-United States d. Great Britian & Ireland, 19-5, Interlachen C.C., Edina, Minn., 1993
12-United States d. Great Britain & Ireland, 18-6, Quaker Ridge G.C., Scarsdale, N.Y., 1997
10-United States d. Great Britain & Ireland, 11-1, Chicago G.C., Wheaton, Ill., 1928
10-United States d. Great Britain & Ireland, 11-1, Seattle (Wash.) G.C., 1961

Most Consecutive Matches Won
United States: 9 (1922 to 1936)
United States: 9 (1947 to 1963)
United States: 8 (1973 to 1987)

4/u

Photo credits